ST. MARTIN'S
TRUE CRIME
CLASSICS

D0770108

EXTRAORDINARY ACCLAIM FOR PETER MEYER AND . . .

St. Martin's True Crime Classics
Titles by Peter Meyer

Blind Love

St Martin's True Crime Library
Titles by Cris Barrish and Peter Meyer

Fatal Embrace

BLIND LOVE

PETER MEYER

St. Martin's Paperbacks

BLIND LOVE

Copyright © 1998, 2000 by Peter Meyer.

Cover photos of David Graham and Diane Zamora by Shelley Katz/ Gamma Liaison; Cover photos of Adrianne Jones by Mark Lazarus; 258 Wolf Run Road, Bartonville, TX 76226, copyright © 1995 by Texas Hot Looks, Inc.; inside photo of Adrianne Jones (in frame) by Mark Lazarus, copyright © 1995 by Texas Hot Looks, Inc.

ISBN: 0-312-96412-9

Printed in the United States of America

St. Martin's Paperbacks edition/January 1998

10 9 8 7 6 5 4

ACKNOWLEDGMENTS

Many people contributed to making this book possible, and I greatly appreciate their cooperation, advice and criticism. Not everyone who helped can be mentioned—they will, I hope, recognize their contributions and accept my thanks—but I can specifically thank various friends and family of the Grahams and Zamoras; Texas police, law enforcement, and government officials; Air Force and Naval Academy officials; fellow journalists and various Mansfield and Crowley residents: Charlie Allen, Mike Androvett, Vickie Bane, Cindy Bean, Laraine Bethke, Alicia Brooks, Dee Davey, Wayne Foreman, Gary and Vickie Foster, Gloria Franco, Jay Green, John Green, Connie Guel, Skip Hollandsworth, Nancy Huckaby, Lt. Commander Patrick M. McCarthy, Tim Madigan, Anne Maier, Blondy Malone, Mike Parrish, Alan Patton, Ellise Pierce, Bonnie Redin, Karen Roebuck, Chuck Sager, Damon Steele, Carlton Stowers, Shakey Texan, Darrell Thompson and Novella Young. Without their assistance, in large and small ways, this book would not have been possible. The mistakes, of course, are my own.

I owe a special debt to both Evie Thompson and Tom Nugent for their valuable research contributions, to my editor Charles Spicer and his assistant Stephen Murphy for shepherding the manuscript, as well as to friends and family—Ed and Lil Linfante, Bonnie Smith, Martin Gross, and Janet and Dylan—for their soothing and steadfast support.

Outside my open window, frogs and crickets made the silence more profound. A chill breeze rustled dead leaves in the woods. It carried an odor of fresh-turned dirt, drawing my attention to the fields where the tractor had only a few hours ago stopped plowing the earth. I sensed the radiance of it in the stillness, sensed the earthworms that burrowed back into the depths of the furrows, sensed the animals that wandered in the woods in search of nocturnal rut or food. I felt the beginning of loneliness, the terrible dread of what I had decided to do.

—John Howard Griffin, *Black Like Me*

Prologue

ROMEO & JULIET
OR
BONNIE & CLYDE?

The Truth About True Crime

"It's a modern-day Romeo and Juliet—*only they kill someone else instead of each other."*

—Television producer

The hardest thing for some people to accept was the fact that the killers had lived among them for almost a year after the murder. For 270 days, after they left Adrianne Jones's body in the weeds, David Graham and Diane Zamora attended classes, went to football games and movies, had their pictures taken by yearbook photographers, were feted by fellow students, praised by local reporters and smiled at by family members who fawned over their celebrity as prospective academy cadets—as if nothing had happened.

Without a confession, blurted one night in a Naval Academy dormitory room, the show may have continued indefinitely. And when the curtain finally came crashing down, so too did all manner of assumptions about who these bright shining stars were. "It couldn't be," was a refrain heard constantly after Graham and Zamora were charged with the murder of Adrianne Jones.

But the single big lie that the couple lived for those nine months seemed to make it difficult for people to remember them accurately. The murder had changed everything, they seemed to imply, including the facts.

Some part of Diane Zamora's past surely propelled her to achieve the greatness that won her a Naval Academy appointment; another part of that past, however, pushed her to something quite different. And was the same gene that thrust David Graham to prominence also implicated in his descent into evil?

At the heart of most of the reports about the arrest of Graham and Zamora were not facts but questions. Questions about who planned the murder and who pulled the trigger; questions about motive and means. Mostly, they ran like veins to a central quarry: why would two young people with so much going for them throw it all away?

This book is meant as an early inquiry into that question. Because it was largely written before Graham and Zamora went to trial, this book necessarily leaves some truths unexplored; however, the fact that two separate juries would find Diane and David guilty of murder speaks volumes about the facts that I report here—and their relevance, on many levels, to the meaning of Adrianne Jones's tragic death. The lengthy and detailed confessions of both suspects, for instance, were helpful in my reconstructing the specific events surrounding the murder; those confessions were later deemed admissible at trial and relied on heavily by jurors in making their judgments about the two former academy cadets' guilt. In any case, every effort has been made to ensure the accuracy of the facts reported; no characters or scenes have been invented, and all dialogue has been constructed from primary or secondary sources. Two names have been changed; in every other respect, it is a work of nonfiction.

In that regard, a word must be said about "the media" coverage of Adrianne Jones's death. Not every murder has the attentions of the *New York Times* and *People* magazine; of *Prime Time Live* and *Current Affair;* of book writers and made-for-television movie producers. In the media, the case enjoyed both a measure of seriousness and seediness.

Not surprisingly, there were complaints from all quarters. The mother of the victim as well as the alleged murderer protested the media's relentless, often harsh, gaze. From jail David Graham exhorted a friend ''not to believe *ANYTHING* you see or hear from the media, because they're full of *CRAP*!!!''

No doubt even killers worry about how they are portrayed in the press. And much of the criticism is a result of numbers: one phone call from a reporter after your daughter is killed is an annoyance; hundreds of calls is an affliction. By the same token, the correct reporting by ten journalists may not overcome the wrong-headedness of a single docudrama.

That is what happened in this case.

Traditionally, journalists journey to places not accessible to everyone—farflung courtrooms and private living rooms, football fields and battlefields, crime scenes and scenes of disaster—and try to accurately report what they see. But in a world of 100-channel televisions, the path to the so-called inaccessible place often looks like an eight-lane highway. Now, there is not just a single knock on a door, but battering rams of tabloid television producers, docudramatists, newspaper reporters, magazine reporters, book writers, television newscasters, lights, cameras, satellite dishes—the works.

This is not too remarkable, except for the toll the trend takes on the patience and goodwill of the subjects of the story—and the facts. Whether because of too many competitive members of the communications media or simply an overstimulated cultural appetite for meaning, the traditional race to get "the story" has turned into a frantic rush to judgment. Facts get trampled—or turned into something else.

The murder of Adrianne Jones and the media attention paid to the arrest of Diane Zamora and David Graham for that murder illustrates the phenomenon. And at the heart of the question of fact and fiction, in this case, is a made-for-television movie:

Love's Deadly Triangle: The Texas Cadet Murder read:

> *What you are about to see is based on an extensive article by Skip Hollandsworth in* Texas Monthly, *other news articles, independent research, and published excerpts from David Graham's written confession.*

Though roundly criticized for airing just five months after Graham and Zamora's arrest—many months before a trial—what was most troubling about NBC's movie was its use and abuse of facts.

The "based-on" claim rings hollow since scenes, dialogue, and even characters are invented without telling the viewer what is real and what isn't. Such invention knows no precedent in traditional journalism. And it did not come from the *Texas Monthly* article, an example of journalism at its best.

However, the makers of docudramas often claim the moral high road. "I hope a lot of teenagers watch it because there are a lot of relatable things going on that could make an impact on them," said

Lindy DeKoven, NBC's senior vice president for movies, about *Love's Deadly Triangle.*

The best lies, as David Graham and Diane Zamora found out, are those sprinkled with facts. But while the piling of fictions onto facts may make for good entertainment, to call the result nonfiction is still a lie.

"The news story substitutes for a plot and the writers feel free to put imagined dialogue into real people's mouths," editorialized the *New York Times* on the day the movie aired. "Violence and sex that would seem gratuitous in fiction can be justified as an educational experience—'a cautionary tale.'"

The commercialization of crime is no sin; distorting the facts is. And though the urge to give life to a story is a powerful one, a seamless narrative need not do disservice to the facts.

This book is an attempt to tell the story of a remarkable crime. It owes a great deal to the reporting of working journalists—not for a story line or a plot device, but for facts—who were there when memories were fresh and who often described events as they happened. But this writer also visited Texas, interviewed dozens of sources independently and made every effort to confirm the accuracy of all the information.

In the end, it is a true story.

Peter Meyer
February 11, 2000

1

A KNOCK ON THE WINDOW

It was well past midnight when Jay Green heard rapping at his window. Asleep, and not sure how long the tapping had been going on, he moved toward the sound, almost mechanically. He didn't have far to go, since he had taken his bed out of the room and slept on the floor.

"Graham," he whispered, as he reached over and popped open the window. He said it "Gram," in a crisp single syllable that showed the traces of his Louisiana origins. "What's goin' on?"

Green reached out and gave David Graham "the P.J.," the handclasp from their para-rescue orientation course.

"You don't wanna know," said Graham as he clambered into the room.

The window opened onto a quiet residential street in Burleson, Texas, a straight 20 miles south of Fort Worth on I-35. Graham had been through it many times and knew the drill. Knock. Pop the screen. Climb in. Put the screen back. Green's parents agreed to look the other way while friends came and went through their son's "front door," as long as the screen was put back up. Usually, it wasn't this late.

"What's goin' on?" Green asked again, as his friend stood up. The two crew-cut teenagers were lean and muscled from their ceaseless exercising.

"I need to stay," said Graham. "Zamora's here too."

Graham reached back and helped Diane Zamora climb through the window. She was a slim, dark-haired girl more than a foot shorter than the 6' 2" Graham. Like Green and Graham, she was a Civil Air Patrol cadet and also, contrary to military decorum, Graham's new love interest.

Zamora mumbled something to Graham and quickly slid into the shadows as Green plugged in the lights to his corner Christmas tree, bathing the small bedroom in an eerie red and green glow.

It was only December 4, but even Texas had Christmas coming and Jay Green, anxious to get in the holiday spirit, had thrown up the scraggly little plastic tree that he had carried with him from military school. He decorated it with shaving cream and, in place of a star on top, gently laid a model of a C-130 transport plane.

Even at 16, Green's life, like Graham's, who had turned 18 the month before, was all military. The two had met at the Civil Air Patrol, an Air Force organization that trained teenagers for military careers. Graham, who had been in C.A.P. since he was 12 and was in line to receive the Spaatz Award, the prestigious honor the national military organization gave, was headed to the Air Force Academy. But

Green, who dreamed of nothing but being a Marine, was worried that his best friend was blowing it.

Just two weeks earlier Graham had been relieved of his Civil Air Patrol command by adult officers.

Now this post-midnight visit.

"We were never here, okay?" said Graham emphatically. "If anyone asks, we were never here."

"What's goin' on?" asked Green.

"You don't want to know," Graham repeated. "Don't ask any questions. We were never here. This never happened."

Green looked at Zamora. "David, it hurts," she said to Graham. She was rubbing her right hand, still heavily bandaged from the September accident in which she wrecked Graham's pickup truck—and nearly lost her life. As far as Green was concerned, Zamora was a large cause of his friend's problems. With apirations of being an astronaut, Zamora had also joined the Civil Air Patrol. Everything was fine until that hot Tuesday evening a few months before, when Graham and Zamora began nudging each other affectionately at a C.A.P. meeting. Now they were engaged to be married.

"It's going to be okay," Graham told Zamora, Then he turned to Green. "Can we stay for a while?"

"Okay. Okay," Green nodded. "Sure."

Graham was, after all, his commanding officer as well as best friend. With their fellow cadet Joseph Uekusa, they had shared many a good time over the last couple of years and Green considered Graham as close as a brother. "We were all on the same wavelength," Green would recall. "We all knew what we were going to do with our lives." All they dreamed of was living lives of patriotic duty—Graham in the Air Force, Green and Uekusa in the Marines—as members of anti-narcotics and covert operations teams fighting evil in South America, the Middle East and Asia. "Uekusa was so hardcore," said Green, "he considered the Air Force a civilian branch of government."

David, who had a pilot's license at age 14, wanted to join the American equivalent of the British Special Air Service, the elite of the elite in counterterrorism. "He always talked about how he'd some day be flying me and Uekusa in to some covert place and drop us off and leave us," said Green. And Green and Uekusa wanted nothing more than to be dropped off in the jungles of enemy territory.

While roaming the back roads in Graham's old pickup truck or sitting around tables in the Brahms Diner or the Dairy Queen, the three discussed the world's hotspots, allowing the Irish Republican Army a grudging respect for fighting against British imperialism and hating drug lords for poisoning America's youth. They considered themselves hard realists about the world and girded themselves for that. They made themselves good with guns—collected them, cleaned them, fired them—and hardened their bodies with constant push-ups and sit-ups, miles of running in the rain, sleeping in bags on hard floors.

Next to Green's sleeping bag was a wall of floor-to-ceiling shelves that held mostly the stuff of battle—knives, ammunition, rope, gas masks, an AK-47 pouch, aerospace manuals—much of it belonging to David Graham, who, except for the last couple of months, seemed to spend as much time at Green's house as his own.

The younger teen now motioned toward a section of the carpeted floor near his small writing desk, just a couple feet from his own sleeping bag. "Sure, stay if you want," he said.

Green hadn't seen Graham for a few weeks, itself an indication of how things had changed lately. But Graham hadn't been himself ever since the summer, when he returned from a week-long international cadet exchange program in Ottawa. He had lost his virginity to a Royal Australian Air Force cadet named "Helen" and for weeks could talk about nothing else. And no sooner had Green and Uekusa convinced him that he couldn't carry on a love affair from halfway around the world—"Graham, why don't you find someone who at least lives in the States?" Green had laughed—Graham took up with Zamora, which had even more serious consequences.

"For one thing, she was an N.C.O.," recalled Green, "a noncommissioned officer, so there was a conflict in rank. Besides that, he was her commanding officer. A lot of times she'd just not do stuff because she could get away with it."

Worse, Graham lost his edge. He started skipping C.A.P. meetings and haircuts. He began wearing rings—not trinkets, but gaudy things that cost $50 and $100 at the mall—and rock music T-shirts. He outfitted his beat-up pickup with $2000 worth of new stereo equipment, paid for with his dad's credit card, bought a pager and, for a few weeks, was calling Green from a new cellular phone. And he became irresponsible with guns. He fired off one of his Russian-made machine guns in his front yard and once put a hole through the floor of his bedroom with one; he especially liked his 9-mm Russian Makarov pistol, which he had begun to carry around with him. Green remembered the time he and Uekusa took the firing pin out of the Makarov as a joke.

"He and Zamora went out with it," Green recalled, "and he came back really mad. He didn't think it was so funny. He said some wild dogs came up on them and he was going to shoot them, but couldn't. It was pretty strange."

It was a remarkable transformation for the ramrod-straight boy who carried the flag to the middle of the Mansfield High football field at halftime and whom Green and Uekusa counted on to figure out what to do in a crisis. These days Graham seemed to be doing just fine creating his own crises.

One of the last times Green had seen his friend was the month before, when Graham returned from the regional cross-country competition in Lubbock, talking not about the race, but of another sexual conquest. "He told me that he had gotten it on with a girl from the track meet," recalled Green. "But I didn't know who she was or where she was from. He just said things got a little crazy."

But by then, Green had stopped paying attention.

Graham was going off the deep end. Losing his C.A.P. command twelve days earlier, a threat to Graham's lifelong Air Force dream, should have straightened him, Green thought.

Instead, Graham was standing in Green's bedroom at two o'clock in the morning, a few weeks before Christmas, insisting, "We were never here."

Green wondered if his friend hadn't finally gotten in trouble with the law. Graham had taken to speeding the backroads, 60, 70, 80 miles an hour, drinking beer and partying. Maybe he'd peeled out in front of some cop and needed to hide out; didn't want his parents to know.

Leaving the lights to his tree on, Green lay back down on his bag on the floor while Graham and Zamora tiptoed across the hallway to the bathroom. Green could hear the water running.

A few moments later Graham came back in the bedroom and asked if he could borrow a pair of shorts. Graham had on a pair of jeans and a gray track shirt, but Green couldn't see much in the holiday light.

"Don't ask," said Graham again, guessing what his friend was thinking. "We were never here. This never happened."

"Okay, sure. That's cool," said Green again, handing a pair of his black shorts to Graham, who went back to the bathroom.

The pair was running water for what seemed like 30 minutes. When they finally returned to the bedroom, Graham was wearing the shorts, but hadn't changed his shirt. The two lay right down beside

Green's desk. No pad, no blanket. Graham wrapped
his arm around Zamora, who was shivering—then
sobbing.

Green was just beginning to doze off when Graham got up. "We gotta go," he said.

Green went to the window, gave Graham another
P.J. and said good-bye.

"Remember, this never happened," he said.
"This is classified. Top secret. Okay?"

"Yeah," said Green. "So, put my screen back
on."

"Thanks, man. You're my best friend."

The next morning Green went in to the bathroom
to make sure his friends hadn't left a mess. He was
concerned there would be bandages or dirt lying
around. But the room was clean. Graham never returned Green's shorts and Green never asked about
them. Top secret. None of them ever talked about
that night again.

2

A BODY

The alarm clock that Monday morning seemed harsher and earlier than usual. But Vickie Foster rolled out of bed at 5:30, as she always did on weekday mornings. She didn't have to leave for work until 8:00, but she needed to accompany her son Zachary to the end of the driveway to wait for the school bus at 6:15.

It was still dark at that hour—a deep-country, December dark, with no street lights, often no starlight and no moon. The sun wouldn't be up for another hour. The bus rolled down the narrow two-lane piece of blacktop that passed less than a hundred yards from the house. Vickie would not let Zachary, starting his freshman year at the regional high school in Mansfield, ten miles away, stand alone in that graveled gloom, no matter how quiet and peaceful it seemed.

There were too many things that went bump in the night in these parts, especially since Joe Pool Lake was built and Dallas and Fort Worth inched closer; drunks and miscreants seemed to stumble onto their property, little more than a patch of nothing on a little lane winding around the scrub. Mostly, the intruders drank or smoked and sometimes knocked the Fosters' fences down, which meant the cattle would get out to roam and, sometimes, become roadkill—in the process becoming the ruination of some poor neighbor's pickup.

Vickie didn't ever want to take the chance that one of these provincial vandals would stumble upon Zachary or he upon them. So after breakfast every school morning she walked him—or drove him—down the gravel driveway to Seeton Road.

And she waited until the doors of the bus closed behind her son and the taillights trailed off before heading back to the house to rouse her husband from bed.

Gary Foster felt more tired than usual when Vickie called to him. Taking advantage of unseasonably warm weather, he and his uncle had hauled hay the previous evening and he now had to fight the urge to crawl deeper under the covers to soothe his muscles. It took a while to muster his big frame out of bed and shuffle it into the shower.

After ten years in a cramped and creaky mobile home, it felt good to finally have a real man's house, with a real man's shower. He and Vickie had bought their sixteen-and-a-third acres of paradise in 1981, and lived in the trailer while they paid off the land. That took what seemed like an eternity; then they had to save for the house. At least, because Gary was an architect, he could design it himself. And he did. It rose, rocklike, from the middle of a field a few dozen yards from the trailer. He could keep an eye on it as it became the full-throated, two-story stone-and-clapboard dwelling that he had drawn; a modest castle with cathedral-ceilinged living room cozied by a large stone fireplace; a house that suited the 6' 2", 220-pound Foster: a big, gentle man and a big, gentle house. At age 45, he felt he deserved it. And it was now so new that shoes were not allowed on the cream-colored living-room carpet.

By seven o'clock Gary had sloshed down a cup of coffee and read the newspaper.

The partial-birth abortion ban was moving to the Senate and the first American troops were about to enter Bosnia. The big news this morning was the Cowboys' loss to the Washington Redskins the day before. In Texas, football was to the 20th century what cattle had been to the 19th: king.

But farming was more important in this section of Texas; nearby Mansfield was founded by a hardy stock of Scottish and Irish millers and as early as 1860 the town had Texas's first steam-powered grist mill.

Though he was born and raised just a mile down the road, one of five children of a crop farmer who had cultivated the land in the area for nearly fifty years, Gary Foster was now one of many of the valley's residents who commuted to a job in the city—Dallas or Fort Worth or Arlington—the bustling economic corridor that had spread into once-empty land making bedroom communities out of former cowtowns. In fact, Gary moved to this parcel when the Army Corps of Engineers took his old house—as they did the homes and lands of dozens of others—to create Joe Pool Recreation Area, the 10-square-mile lake and park the state created to help serve the sports and recreational needs of the surging population.

Gary finished his coffee and said good-bye to his wife. He had a drive to his draftsman's job with the buildings department of Zell, the large jewelry retailer.

Outside, the morning was calm. A vulture drifted across the sky, head cocked in search of roadkill. The dark country nights usually yielded their share of doomed souls caught in the headlights of speeding cars.

To the west, signs of the population encroachment were visible from Foster's lot, from which he could see the giant television and radio towers glistening on top of nearby Cedar Hill and the roofs of some of the hillside's new million-dollar homes. There was now even a marina, a country club and a golf course rolling through the nearby trees to the north.

To the south, acreage-for-sale signs seemed as prolific as the soybean fields from which they sprouted. When Foster was small, the farmers were growing cotton and corn; now, they were raising mostly maize, wheat and corn and only small amounts of cotton.

The small town of Mansfield, a half-dozen miles to the west, was spreading development tentacles in all directions. Big brick houses, like the one Gary Foster himself had built, were popping up everywhere. The most popular issues before the town council concerned development, road construction, utility fees and crime. The population had nearly tripled in ten years, from 8,000 to 22,000; Baptist churches shared space with strip malls; fields of wildflowers ran up to McDonald's. In one recent month there were nearly 40 new home permits issued, worth an average of $150,000 each. The Mansfield school district, which pulled in kids from towns throughout the region, was one of the top 50 employers in the area, tied with Union Pacific Railroad, and was reporting an increased number of calls from prospective residents.

Population brought crime and this morning's newspaper was a reminder of how things had changed over the years. Another front-page story announced that Texas was leading the nation in prison growth by spending $2 billion, building 100,000 new prison beds the previous four years. And in the "Metro" section were stories that helped explain why the state was building new prisons. "Body without hands, head baffles Dallas authorities," was the lead story on this December 4 morning.

That May the town council had voted to put a half-cent sales tax increase—from 7.75 percent to 8.25 percent—before the voters; most of the extra revenue, said Mayor Duane Murray, would go toward beefing up the police force in town. "As we're growing," said Mansfield Chamber of Commerce Manager Shirley Karznia, "we've got to increase the police department."

No doubt, Mansfield had its share of peace and tranquility. But the postcard view of Main Street—with its two- and three-story brick buildings, and a local weekly paper that ran stories about garage sales and fish fries, cub scout meetings and well-baby immunization programs—covered a rich vein of violence and tumult.

There was no monument to Mansfield's most famous citizen, John Howard Griffin, author of *Black Like Me,* perhaps because its most famous event was a week-long race riot in 1956—by whites. "This would be a horrible way to die," was the sign on an effigy of a black person strung to a downtown utility pole back then. "This Negro tried to enter a white school." Mansfield was one of the first school districts in the country to defy a federal integration order. But the town also had its "Harmony," a small enclave on the town's western fringe, created by a town father to give safe haven to freed slaves.

It was now light and most of what Gary Foster could see from his front door was pretty much like the farm and cattle country of his youth: open land, punctuated by stands of scrub trees and farm houses and fields fenced by barbed wire.

Across a grassy field to the west, a few hundred yards away, Gary could see his mother's new house, vacant, up for sale. He could see some of his cattle—he now had sixteen head that he raised for some extra money—beginning their quotidian chew and chaw, heads bobbing, hooves inching through

the grass. He gave a cursory glance toward the di-
lapidated out-buildings on the southern edge of his
parcel on Seeton Road. He didn't use them for much
except storing tools and had to keep watch for vandals.

He drove down his gravel driveway, past the
small pond his cattle used for drinking, and turned
right onto Seeton Road. On his left was the outer
edge of the Joe Pool Lake recreation area, but here
it didn't look very recreational: scrub brush, briars,
weed trees and a string of barbed wire barred anyone but the determined trespasser from entry. He
pulled up at a string of mailboxes on the park's
perimeter on the left to deposit an envelope. He
didn't have to worry about oncoming traffic on this
lonely stretch of road.

He couldn't help but glance to his right to admire
his new house in the small clearing up the hill, beyond the small piece of ground they sometimes used
as a garden and the crumbling old shed they stored
old tools in. But as he did, he also noticed that the
barbed-wire gate to his field was disturbed. This
was nothing new to Gary. In fact, since late-night
loiterers seemed drawn to the weatherbeaten shack
just beyond the little patch of grass on the other side
of his gate, he had made a point of driving by this
spot every morning to make sure the fence was
closed. It was a lot easier shutting a gate, he knew
from experience, than chasing down some cows.

He and his uncle had used the gate to drive the
pickup in and out of the field the night before, but
he was sure he had pulled the gate shut when they

finished. Now it was askew, bowed slightly and dragged inward. It wasn't a pretty gate, but it worked to keep the cattle in—and most trespassers out. Six strands of tough barbed wire, a foot apart, were hitched to a vertical post in the ground on the right side of the 15-foot opening and, in the same equidistant measure, the other ends of the strands were tied to a slim, five-foot-long metal stake. The stake, however, was not in the ground, but served as a long handle, with which to pull the metal lines taut across the opening. To secure it, Foster simply planted one end of the stake in the ground against an in-ground post, then pulled on the top of the stake until it touched the larger post. Then he looped a wire over the two uprights, holding them together. By weaving a couple more pieces of the sharp wire between the horizontal strands, Foster had himself a good gate—easy enough to throw open, but strong enough to thwart a persistent bull. It was a common gate in cattle country—easy to make, and mean.

Foster put his car in gear to drive forward to fix the gate. But as he did he noticed something else. At first glance it looked like a slight lump on the grass just beyond the gate. But as he focused his gaze, he realized it was a human figure.

Instinctively, he looked left and right, glancing also in the rearview mirror, doublechecking that the car doors were locked. This could be a trap, he thought. The woman—now he was sure it was a woman—was bait, meant to lure him out of his car so he could be jumped by accomplices hiding in the bushes.

For a time Foster did nothing. The morning was as still as if the woman weren't there. The cattle were still chewing. White wisps of smoke were puffing from a couple of chimneys. A bird breezed by. Nothing was out of the ordinary—except for this figure on the ground beyond the gate. That scared him.

Foster inched the car forward, pulling up even with the gate and the woman prostrate on the grass just behind it. She was wearing a white sweatshirt and plaid shorts, lying on her back, arms at her sides, looking up, it seemed, as if she had simply lay down to take in the sweet sky on a fragrant summer's afternoon. Only it wasn't summer and it wasn't afternoon.

Her hair was blond, her skin was white, her white-stockinged feet pointed balletlike forward. In the early morning light, with the dew still glistening slightly atop the trampled blades of grass and the three-foot stand of weeds running along each side of the grassy tractor trail, she looked like an angel dropped from the sky, floating peacefully on a bed of earth—and unfortunately held in place by a single barb of wire that tugged on the toe of her right stocking, a hint that this was not God's work, but the devil's.

Foster knew now: the woman was dead. Dead. His heart raced. He had never seen a dead body except at funerals. And part of him still could not believe that the life was gone from this girl.

He could see blood on her face. He could feel his own heart beating.

Glancing in the mirror, Foster watched carefully for movement. He then pulled his car ahead to the next driveway, a few dozen yards up the road, turned around and drove back. He could hear the gravel crackle under the wheels as he pulled up to the gate again. Now, looking out from his open car window directly at the woman, he seemed close enough to touch her. She looked no more than 20 years old.

Then another thought disturbed Foster's gaze. Drugs. Someone had killed her and dumped her body here, he thought. But when? She looked so much alive and the blood on her face so bright that Foster thought he may in fact have startled the killers before they had finished doing what they had planned to do. Where were they now?

Foster sped off.

Vickie Foster saw the car gunning up the driveway from her chair in front of the living room television.

"What the hell!" she wondered out loud.

Her husband flew in the front door and raced by her, shouting, "Somebody dumped a body at the garden!"

"What!"

"Somebody dumped a body at the garden!"

"You're kidding?"

"No."

By now Foster was punching buttons on the phone in the kitchen.

First, it was 911. He identified himself, explained what he had found and where he was. After he hung up, Foster immediately made another call—to his cousin, a Dallas policeman who lived just down the road. If past experience was any guide, he knew how long it might take the local police to find his farm. He explained to his cousin his fear that the murderers were still in the area.

"I might have just scared them off," he said. Vickie was now standing next to him. Killers? Here? Now? "I don't know what's going on."

Foster asked his cousin if he could meet him at the gate and wait with him until the police came.

He headed back to his car—his wife right on his elbow. They pulled up to the site, across the road and waited for Foster's cousin. When the other man got there, Foster finally got out of his car and approached the gate on foot. All three people now stared over the fence at the lifeless form in the grass a few feet away.

"It was almost like she was posed," recalled Gary.

"Like they placed her that way," said Vickie.

"You wouldn't think she'd just fall that way, but I suppose anything is possible."

"I don't see how you're going to turn around and fall flat on your back like that," Vickie later remarked. "But I guess it's possible. Anything's possible. I wasn't about to go up to her."

"It was one of those deals where you didn't want to look," recalled Gary, "but you had to because you knew you'd be asked questions about what it looked like. So you wanted to look enough to be able to describe it, yet—even looking at her, we missed details. We were just shocked.''

Vickie averted her eyes. ''It was a weird, eerie feeling, seeing someone lying there, knowing they're not going to get up. The first thing I thought,'' she recalled, ''is 'That's somebody's kid.' ''

3

A MISSING GIRL

Barely thirty minutes after Vickie Foster rose that morning, Linda Jones, in nearby Mansfield, was awakened by the insistent ringing of the alarm clock in her daughter's bedroom.

What was wrong with Adrianne? Annoyed, Linda got up, padded down the hall and turned the time-piece off.

Where was Adrianne? It wasn't like her not to be here. Linda guessed that she had gotten up early, forgotten about the clock and was now out walking the dogs or running. A knee injury had forced Adrianne off the high school's soccer team, but the athletic sixteen-year-old had joined the cross-country squad, took exercise classes and loved to jog, often running to and from her after-school job at the Golden Fried Chicken drive-in restaurant almost a mile away. Her cross-country team had qualified for the regional meet in Lubbock a few weeks before and she was waiting for her "letterman" jacket.

Linda looked around the bedroom for a moment. It was a teenager's pad, with soccer posters on the wall, a Mickey Mouse phone and music—Adrianne's favorites were Pearl Jam, Annie Lennox and the techno-rave 2 Unlimited—that she played on the stereo which next-door neighbor and best friend Jessica Ramon had sold her for ten dollars. The level-headed young woman's biggest extravagance was her waterbed, which, Linda now noticed, was made. She also saw that Adrianne's running shoes were still there.

When Adrianne did not arrive for her ride to school at eight that morning, Linda called the police. This was completely out-of-character for her daughter. Yes, she often tested her parents' patience with a rambunctious spirit and minor rebellions. And, yes, lately, she had been slipping out of the house at night to visit friends and "party." And, yes, her father, Bill Jones, a crusty and plain-spoken heavy equipment mechanic, had nailed shut the window of Adrianne's bedroom when he caught her. But she would never stay out all night or miss school.

The popular and pretty Mansfield High School sophomore, already pegged by some as a cheerleader, was also an honors student, took advanced courses, studied at least two hours a night and was already planning to go to Texas A&M University to become a veterinarian.

Bill Jones had moved his family—including Adrianne and her two younger brothers—from Dallas to Mansfield in 1984, in search of a safe place to raise his children. At the time, the town was quiet and peaceful, close enough to Dallas and Fort Worth to make bigger cities accessible, but far enough away to be able to hear birds sing or to walk to fields of grazing cattle.

But his daughter's growing independence co-incided with the growth of a metropolitan region, now referred to as if it were one city, "Dallas–Fort Worth," and known locally as the Metroplex.

Bill Jones was not about to let down his guard as his daughter matured. It was only that autumn, the beginning of her sophomore year, that he had allowed Adrianne to stay out past nine o'clock on weekends. And he made her produce receipts if she said she was going to the movies. But he had also found a way to his daughter's heart, and the two were restoring a vintage 1940s-era Ford pickup truck.

"I truly felt that if we had some rules that kept her away from teenage temptations," he would later say, "we'd be okay."

So where was Adrianne now? Linda called the Golden Fried Chicken drive-in, where Adrianne had worked the previous evening, and Mansfield High School, to see if anyone had seen her. No one had.

Linda was now trying to remember everything that happened the day before.

Adrianne had worked the evening shift at Golden Fried while Linda had spent most of Sunday paint-ing the bedroom. She was in bed watching televi-sion when Adrianne got home from work, about nine o'clock. She had put in a four-hour shift that day. But instead of running home, as she often did, Adrianne hitched a ride from one of the restaurant's delivery drivers and wanted to go work out.

A crazy idea, but not surprising from Adrianne, who seemed to have boundless energy. She asked her mother to drive her to Huguley's Fitness Center, only about fifteen minutes away, on I-35. This was one of the advantages of the metropolitan incursion on the once remote area: a 24-hour exercise club.

Linda, a massage therapist at the Serendipity beauty salon on Main Street, agreed to go work out with her daughter.

It was after ten when mother and daughter were driving home, and Linda would recall that Adrianne was in a particularly thoughtful mood that night. She began talking about what she might do with her life and what career she would pursue.

"I want to be able to determine how people act the way they do, Mom," she told her mother. "What is a person who does that?"

"A behavioral analyst," said Linda. "That's somebody who takes you aside, studies you, and gives you an analysis of why you behave like you do, and you kind of set them on the right path and get them going."

"That is what I want to be," Adrianne announced.

And her mother knew she would be damn good at it. Not only smart, Adrianne was blessed with an infectiously gregarious personality and an unpretentious, hazel-eyed radiance that was already beginning to draw boys to the Joneses' Walnut Creek ranch home—even if just to drive by and hope to see her lounging on the front yard.

Jessica Ramon recalled the evenings that she and

A. J., as her friends called her, set up lawn chairs on the edge of Jessica's yard just to visit with friends who passed. And if no one came by, the two girls had no trouble entertaining themselves. "She just made herself laugh by being silly," recalled Jessica. "I'd say, 'Walk like Michael Jackson,' and she'd try her hardest to do a moonwalk, but she was not a very good dancer. She wasn't coordinated. No rhythm. No body movement. But she didn't care what anybody thought."

Adrianne would sometimes wear her favorite flower-patterned, long blue dress, tied at the back of her neck, without shoes. "She'd say, 'There are no shoes good enough to go with this dress,' " Jessica recalled.

A free spirit, at work A. J. drew a smiley face on her Golden Fried visor, joked with customers and shot spitballs through straws at coworkers. "She was my superstar employee," said Tina Dollar, manager of the restaurant. "I made her the cashier at the drive-through window because she knew how to put a smile on everyone's face. . . . After taking an order, she'd say funny things to the customers like, 'Okay, drive forward to the ninety-ninth window to get your food!' "

She was, said her friend Tracy Bumpass, a "big flirt," who met her current boyfriend at the Golden Fried. "I'm sure lots of guys really liked Adrianne," recalled Sydney Jones, a friend and former soccer teammate. "She was the kind of girl who would say hi to you in the hallway at school even if you didn't know her."

Who didn't like her?

"She always uplifted everyone around her," said Tina Dollar.

Adrianne had inherited her mom's blond hair and her independent spirit and the two were best friends. "Bubble butt," Linda would jokingly call her daughter, a reference to Adrianne's well-toned backside; an acknowledgment also of her daughter's budding sexuality. Her mother would give her a hard time for taking two hours to put makeup on so that it looked like she wasn't wearing makeup.

"When I asked her why she went to such trouble to put her makeup on before she went out of the house," Linda recalled, "she said, 'Mom, you never know who you might meet.'"

Linda had recently treated Adrianne to a photo session at a local studio in which the young woman, hair teased to a lustrous glow around her soft face, slipped into sleeveless gowns with plunging necklines, donned bejeweled earrings and stared confidently at the camera. Though her mom was planning on giving Adrianne the glamour shots as a joke for Christmas, she was also proud of her daughter's poise.

Mother and daughter had just walked in the door, at 10:45 P.M., when the phone rang.

"Who the hell is that?" said Linda as her daughter picked up the handset.

It was for Adrianne. Linda told her daughter to hang up, that it was too late to be on the phone, but Adrianne signaled that it was Tracy Smith, her new boyfriend, who had just gotten back from a week-end away with his parents.

Besides, Tracy, a big kid from the nearby town of Venus, didn't go to Mansfield High, so Linda was more indulgent of the late-night phone call. Linda told her daughter that she could speak for just a few minutes.

Adrianne dawdled, even walking down the hall with the portable handset to put a load of laundry in the washing machine as she talked. She took another call with the call-waiting service while on the phone with Tracy.

"Who was that?" Linda asked about the second caller.

"It was David from cross-country," said Adrianne. "He's upset about something." Linda didn't know who that was, but she thought that Adrianne seemed "antsy" after the phone call.

"Well, get your butt to bed," said Linda. "I'm tired."

Though open and honest about most things, Adrianne Jones did not tell her mom about David Graham, the good-looking senior at Mansfield High whom she had met on the cross-country team that fall.

It was one of the least sexy sports in Texas high school, where football was king, and the small group of athletes didn't draw much attention to themselves. Neither did the budding friendship between Graham and Jones attract much attention.

The tall, blond, muscular David was one of the most eligible young men at Mansfield.

"You know how growing up, your mom tells you about the perfect guy, the perfect gentleman, and there's nobody out there like that?" recalled Sarah Layton, a schoolmate of Graham's at Mansfield High. "David was. He was one of the last cool guys on earth."

He was "extremely nice," said another female classmate. Funny, but not overly talkative.

"His life was so unblemished," said one woman who knew him, "that he didn't so much as throw a spitwad in school." David had impeccable academic credentials, ran on the track and cross-country teams and was a battalion commander in Junior ROTC.

But he was not a star athlete or a school government activist. He played football for only a year before deciding he didn't need the physical pain. He was not a "popular" boy, but a respected one, by both boys and girls, despite an ardor for military traditions that often inspired ridicule among other students. "Some of the more sarcastic guys in school would address him as Colonel Graham," recalled Jennifer Skinner, who sat near Graham in a high school government class. "But you could tell they sort of said it out of respect."

Everyone who knew David called attention to the durability of his dream of flying. No one really knew where that obsession came from exactly—only that it had been there for a long time.

Girls liked him because he liked Garfield; they

called him "Chipmunk" because of his gap-toothed smile.

"He was very dependable, very courteous, very businesslike," said Bob Sloate, manager of the Winn-Dixie on Walnut Creek Drive, where David worked part-time, after school. "Everything was 'Yes, sir' and 'No, sir.' "

Some students knew that Graham and Jones spent time together; others, friends of David and Adrianne, didn't.

Tina Dollar, manager of the Golden Fried, remembered Adrianne showing her a small picture that she had in her wallet, saying, "His name is David."

Another friend, Tracy Bumpass, would claim that "Adrianne told me everything, but she never mentioned David."

Their relationship was made more complicated because they, like many young people in the Metroplex region, ranged far beyond the small towns to which they were nominally attached. Adrianne and David's Mansfield school district swept up children from dozens of towns covering over 100 square miles of Tarrant and Johnson counties; the student population was more than half the population of the entire town it was named after. A thirty-minute drive—and most students had cars—could put a kid in the heart of Dallas or Fort Worth, at Great Adventure or a Cowboys game, a rodeo or a rave party.

David's fiancée, Diane Zamora, was a senior at Crowley High School, a dozen miles away to the

west. He saw her only after school. And his two
best friends, Joseph Uekusa and Jay Green went to
Burleson High School, ten miles to the south and
west. He had been seeing them less now that Diane
was on the scene, but he never saw them during the
school day. Secrets were easy. Almost inadvertently, David was falling for another girl; and no
one really knew.

Some students noticed, but no one paid much attention. "He saw her fairly often," recalled one
Mansfield High student, "even if it wasn't what you
would call dating."

"David was kind of reserved," said a fellow
worker at the Winn-Dixie grocery store, where Graham had worked. "But he would tell me he had
some problems with her [Jones] and then he would
say he loved her."

While trying to make up his mind about Adrianne, he found himself on a bus early one Saturday
morning headed to the district cross-country meet
in Lubbock, 250 miles away. Adrianne was there.
Pretty, blond, perky. They talked, they laughed.
After the meet, he and Adrianne talked most of the
long van ride back to Mansfield. It seemed natural
to offer her a lift home from the school parking lot.
He had been driving an old station wagon since Diane had wrecked his pickup truck. Adrianne didn't
have a car.

Though less than a mile to her house, straight
down Walnut Creek Drive, Adrianne asked David
to turn off the main street. She directed him to take
a couple more turns and soon the teens found

themselves parked behind Alice Ponder Elementary School, where David's dad had once been principal. No one was there. Soon the two were having sex in the back of David's station wagon.

It was possible that Adrianne didn't care enough about David Graham to tell anyone; or that the sex they had that afternoon in November meant nothing to her.

Or, if she did know about his engagement to Diane Zamora, perhaps she didn't broadcast her friendship with him because she didn't want a reputation for getting involved with another girl's guy. After all, one of Adrianne's good friends had landed in the hospital the year before for such an indiscretion, beaten nearly to death with a baseball bat wielded by a jealous fourteen-year-old girl.

David, however, told his two best friends immediately. Green didn't seem to pay much attention. To Joseph Uekusa, he said, in their crisp military jargon, "I want you to listen, then forget." He told Uekusa what happened with Adrianne. Then he made him promise not to tell Diane.

"If anyone ever tells Diane," he said, "it will be me."

Though Bill Jones resettled his family in search of a peaceful environment, Mansfield was a town, not unlike many in the last decade of 20th-century America, that had its own share of crime and violence. Though statistically 25 percent safer than Dallas, it still registered one crime for every 16 citizens.

Mansfield had its church steeples and bake sales, but, during the previous month there were 84 adults and nine juveniles arrested, including two robberies, 16 assaults, 113 burglaries, 42 larceny cases and one motor vehicle theft.

One arrest that sent shivers down the spines of most parents in town was that of the 15-year-old boy who brought a .38-caliber revolver to T.A. Howard Middle School. No one was hurt, but, as the weekly *Mansfield News-Mirror* noted, "The incident sparked concern among students, parents and teachers at the campus."

This was not a crime wave so much as a high tide; not enough to keep people up at night as much as make them lock their doors before turning the lights off—or, as Bill Jones did, nail his daughter's window shut, until she could appreciate the risks of the dark. There was no reason to believe that their daughter wouldn't come home—except that she didn't.

Linda got Lee Ann Burke, Mansfield High's cross-country coach, on the phone.

"Adrianne's missing," said Linda. "Is there a David on the cross-country team?"

"Yes," said Burke.

"I think he called her last night," said Linda.

Burke didn't know what to make of Linda Jones's call. She didn't know David and Adrianne were friends. She thought of him as an average cross-country athlete, best known at Mansfield for being one of the uniformed members of the honor guard who marched the flags to the center of the field at football games; battalion commander of the Junior ROTC program who was headed to the Air Force Academy and always said, "Yes, ma'am" and "No, ma'am."

Burke sent April Grossman to David's second-period math class to ask if he had called Adrianne the previous night.

David stared at April as if she were not making sense. "Did I talk to Adrianne?" he responded. "No. Why would I?"

In the meantime, Mansfield police had contacted principal Jerry Kirby, who assigned two of the high school's associate principals to help make calls about Adrianne. "We have kids reported missing quite a bit," Kirby would later say. "Fortunately, in most of the cases the child is back at home that night."

4

A CLENCHED FIST

Gloria Franco was on regular duty that Monday morning, normally a quiet time at the Tarrant County Medical Examiner's Office. Murders tended not to happen on Monday mornings—not like they did on Friday and Saturday nights. And when her phone rang, just before 8:30, she didn't actually expect that it would be a summons to a crime scene.

But the dispatcher from the Grand Prairie police department, 20 miles to the east, had a live one—rather, a dead one. "Body found in a field," Franco noted on her pad. She wrote the essential information, first verifying that the deceased was within her jurisdiction.

But for a line on the map, the case would have fallen to the Mansfield police department—the body was located just a few hundred yards east of the Mansfield town line, in Grand Prairie's jurisdiction, a fact that struck many as odd, since Mansfield's Main Street was only five miles to the west of Gary Foster's house while Grand Prairie's police headquarters was more than ten miles to the north and east.

Some Mansfield residents were sensitive to the jurisdictional question, however, since they still considered that Grand Prairie had pulled a fast one in grabbing land that would become Joe Pool Recreation area, with vacation homes and golf courses. Gary Foster experienced the problem differently: it always took Grand Prairie police forever, it seemed, to find his place when he called them about prowlers.

That fact didn't much matter to Franco, whose territory included both areas.

The Tarrant County M.E. served a wide swath of country: the city of Fort Worth and all the little towns of Tarrant, Parker and Denton Counties. Grand Prairie was one of dozens of police agencies that used the TCMEO to handle its suspicious deaths. In fact, Franco's boss, Nizam Peerwani, had overseen the autopsies from the Waco siege in 1991.

Franco hung up the phone and noted, "It appears body dumped in this location as barbed wire fence in place." This could mean anything, she knew.

Franco grabbed her camera and sketch pad and jumped in one of the two county cars the death investigators used and drove south and east on I-35, the eight-lane freeway that ran along Fort Worth's eastern flank and south across flat, former prairie land toward San Antonio. It was a river of asphalt banked by shopping centers, all-night eateries, Taco Bells and IHOPs, Radio Shacks and used car shacks and American flags as large as fields of grain. But just five miles south and a mile or so east and the parking lots turned to earth, the roads got narrower and cars dirtier. There were now stands of scrub oak and fields with two-ton bales of hay.

After picking her way up and down tiny roads with no names, Franco finally arrived at the Seeton Road scene. There were already a number of police from Grand Prairie, including a crime scene unit, detectives and a patrol unit waiting for her. Franco's title: Forensic Death Investigator. Her jurisdiction was clear: the dead body. A soft-spoken, middle-aged woman with a pretty round face and dark hair, she didn't look like an intrepid sleuth of the lifeless.

In her notebook, she wrote the temperature: 63 degrees. Not the best conditions for the preservation of dead bodies—but better than a hundred.

For the moment, the cops at the scene deferred to Franco, who noted the location of the body: still lying smack in the middle of the grassy lane that Foster and his uncle had driven up the night before while hauling hay.

At first glance there was no sign of a struggle. The girl lay on her back without shoes—suggesting that the body may have been dumped there—just on the other side of the barbed-wire gate, which was mostly closed. There had been a time when most of Grand Prairie murders were "found bodies."

"Back then," said a veteran detective, "it was sort of like wide open space out here, the fringes of nowhere. It was a good area to get rid of a body."

In fact, though Grand Prairie's population had more than doubled in the last twenty years, its murder rate was about the same, explained largely by topography: as open spaces closed, it was no longer a popular place to lose a body in. "Now," said one cop, "they're mostly our own murders."

Mansfield had its own share of problems, including murder. Though it normally would see a homicide only every couple of years, the body on the ground this December morning would be the fifth homicide in as many years.

The body in Foster's field was most likely a teenager, but investigators weren't sure who she was, where she came from or how she got there. The wire gate seemed to have been knocked down and put back up; but the girl's sock was still hooked on one of the barbs, as if she fell over it. Gary Foster said he hadn't touched anything.

On one of the higher wires, a few feet above the ground, another rusty barb held a wad of blond hair, most likely from the victim, who lay just as Foster had found her, on her back, arms to her side, left foot dangling gently from a wire.

But there was no peace in this repose. The fact that the body had no shoes seemed evidence that she had been killed elsewhere, in a house perhaps, loaded into a trunk and driven to this secluded spot. But there were bloody scratch marks on the young woman's white legs, and blood smeared on her left thigh; bleeding that would indicate a beating heart when the injuries occurred. And if, as Franco suspected, they were abrasions from the barbed wire, it would mean the woman was alive as she went through the fence.

Franco snapped pictures and drew a diagram of the scene.

As the investigators probed closer to the body, it was not hard to guess the cause of death: there were two bullet wounds to the head, one right between the eyes. It was as if she had been executed. There was also a huge gash on the side of her head—and large amounts of blood, soaking her long blond hair. The blood, already congealed and dried, had also discolored the white skin of her neck and the two shirts she was wearing. The small hoop earring in her left ear was twisted open and there were bruises on her neck. She had clearly struggled against someone holding her around the neck. But her clothes were not disturbed in a way that would have suggested a sexual assault.

"Rigor complete," Franco noted. "There is a wound to the left cheek and another wound to the middle forehead. Blood is matted in hair and under head. Some brain matter visible to top of head."

This was Franco's job: clinical detail.

Whether it was the blow to the head or the bullets that killed her, it was clear that she had put up a fight. The knuckles of her left hand were bruised and bloodied, as if she had hit something or deflected a blow.

Investigators then saw something more distressing than the bullet wounds. The woman's right hand, resting still on the ground at her side, was clenched. The back of the hand was smeared with blood, as if she had rubbed something, like one would do with wet stinging tears in the eyes, as if she had perhaps wiped away the blood streaming from her head before collapsing here or while lying here, on the wet ground in what was surely the dark of night. And there she must have lain, for some period—a few seconds, a few hours?—alive, for her bloodied hand was grasping a clump of grass, a last lunge for life.

It was not an easy death.

"It takes a cold-blooded person to shoot a pretty young girl in the face from two to four feet away," one cop later remarked. "That girl was mangled and it was sickening to look at."

Franco closed her sketch book and called the Tarrant County mortician to come pick up the body.

5

JANE DOE

They did not have an identification of the young woman they rolled through the back door of the medical examiner's office on the southeast side of Fort Worth. She was tagged Jane Doe, case number 954705T, and put in a refrigerated storage room, to await a medical examiner's probing and, the forensic experts guessed, a quick identification. A healthy young woman, they knew, would be missed.

"The body is clothed in white socks, blue-and-green plaid flannel shorts, a white Nike brand long-sleeved knit shirt over a gray t-shirt bearing a logo 'UIL Region-I Cross-Country Regionals 1995,' floral print underpants and a white metal ball chain on the right ankle," Dr. Marc Krouse dictated, standing over the prostrate form on the slab in the examination room a little after one o'clock that afternoon.

He peeled away the layers of clothing as he proceeded, noting that the socks and t-shirt were torn.

"The body is that of a normally developed, well-nourished and well-hydrated Caucasian adolescent," he said, taking the clinical measurements for the record: she was 5' 3" tall and weighed 116.2

pounds. "The body is well-preserved, unembalmed and cool post refrigeration. Rigor is moderate ongoing to full. Lividity is developed, reduced, dependent, purple and blanchable," noted Krouse, probing and poking.

A photographer took pictures at each stage of the process—forty-nine pictures in all.

"The scalp is covered by moderately long, slightly wavy blond hair. The body hair is female and average. The calvarium [upper skull] is symmetric. There are defects associated with gunshot injuries." The closer Krouse got, the more technical became his monologue. The necessary coolness about the body that was assuredly someone's daughter, sister, niece—it was the only way to get through this dozens of times.

Krouse inspected every inch of the body, leaving little to the imagination, noting what looked normal, as well as what did not, from fingers to toes, eyes to ears. "There is no evidence of genital trauma," Krouse found. "A tampon is in place in the vagina." Though he would need to perform a complete rape exam to be sure, there was no sign of sexual assault.

There were a number of injuries that would have been painful and helped tell a tale of what must have been a fierce struggle: bruises around her jaw and scrapes and bruises on her neck that were consistent with a strangulation attempt that she probably fought her way free of—Krouse could not tell how much the blunt-object injury contributed to the girl's death, but noted that it was "perimortem," had occurred very close in time to her death. The back of her left hand was bruised and the index finger on the same hand was broken. "A series of abrasions and superficial puncture wounds (some with obvious hemorrhage) are found on the legs," he observed. There was a long cut on her left thigh, cuts and bruises on her left knee, as well as cuts on her right knee, shin, calf and foot.

It was a painful struggle, but, at this stage, it was unclear how long it had lasted. The fight surely ended, however, Krouse knew, with the severe trauma to the head. There he found "blood flowing across the face" and dried blood in the nose and mouth, all of it probably from the bullet wounds or the "blunt traumatic head injury," as Krouse called the inch-wide gash above the girl's left ear. That blow shattered the skull and the pathologist now removed bone fragments that were three-quarters of an inch deep, embedded in the brain itself.

That blow could have killed the girl. But, in terms of cause of death, it wouldn't much matter. The bullet wounds, as Krouse found, were precisely and mortally devastating. Four of them: two, cursory exam showed, were most likely entrance and two, exit.

"Wound number one is found over the left malar face centered three inches below the glabella one-and-a-half inches left of midline." If Krouse called the hole in the girl's left cheek "a 5/16-inch diameter skin defect," it was only because he would go on to describe each defect, as the bullet tore through the head. He found "faint powder stippling'' that would have indicated that this was an entry wound and that the shot was to the face—not the back of the head—from close range.

Krouse traced the bullet's path, upward and rightward, exiting the back of her head nearly two inches higher than the point it entered—and wreaking unspeakable havoc as it passed through, as Krouse noted, the nasal cavity, the cranial cavity, the brain's front lobe, several cerebral arteries, the lateral ventricle that carried spinal fluid around the brain and the right frontal lobe, exiting the skull a short few inches from where it entered, but blowing a hole in the side of the girl's head that not only left an inch-and-a-half hole in her skull, but cracked it, sending fracture lines in three different directions across the back of her head from the exit wound.

The shooter must have been close, within a few feet, and below the victim: the angle of the trajectory was steep.

Though he couldn't tell with precision which wound was inflicted first, the second bullet hole was, according to what Krouse found on the external evidence, more vicious and straight in its trajectory. This was the shot between the eyes. Krouse described it as ''stellate'' in shape, starlike; but there was nothing poetic about it—just a small jagged hole, the diameter of a dime, in the middle of the girl's forehead. From a distance, it seemed oddly innocuous, like an unpleasant scab on a pretty face. But Krouse knew it as the shape of sure death. There was also ''light powder stippling'' on this wound, but Krouse, as if anticipating the next question—was the gun pressed to her head?—noted that there was no evidence of any soot within the wound, "nor is there evidence of a muzzle imprint."

That hardly made a difference to the deadly straight course the speeding piece of metal took through the middle of the girl's head—"passing anterior to posterior and slightly inferior to superior and minimally left to right"—destroying brain mass and nerve tissue before exploding out the skull in the back of her head.

Krouse found, "free in the hair," a large caliber bullet and marked it #950182. This would be a crucial piece of evidence in any future legal proceeding, Krouse knew. Other forensic investigators would be able to match the bullet to the murder weapon and, hopefully, find, at least, the gun's owner.

Krouse took a break before proceeding to the part of the autopsy that required the knife. But just before four o'clock that afternoon, before he began, Forensic Death Investigator Franco took a call from Lieutenant Steve Noonkester at the Mansfield police department. Noonkester told Franco that he had a missing person report for a 16-year-old white female who had been missing since the previous evening.

Noonkester told Franco that the girl had a scar on her left knee, a result of some microscopic surgery, and, said Nooncaster, might have been wearing workout or athletic clothes. A Grand Prairie police officer was on his way to the parents' home to pick up a picture of the missing girl and would bring it to Franco's office to see if it matched the body discovered on Seeton Road that morning. If it were the missing girl, said Noonkester, her name was Adrianne Jessica Jones.

Sergeant Craig Magnuson had already guessed the outcome. But he would not tell Linda Jones what he thought. He had come to the Joneses' house as a friend, when he first heard that Adrianne was missing. But, when he heard about the body being found out by Joe Pool Lake—"a young woman"— he was not hopeful about Bill and Linda's only daughter.

Magnuson was at the Joneses' house that afternoon when Noonkester called from the medical examiner's office. Noonkester himself had driven the 20 miles from Mansfield to Fort Worth with the picture of Adrianne. When he arrived, they had to pull Deputy Chief Medical Examiner Krouse out of the middle of the autopsy of the unidentified woman to look at the picture. Krouse nodded.

Magnuson hung up the phone and went to Linda Jones.

"You are like, 'No, no, no, no, no. This is not happening, this is a nightmare,' " she would recall. "The thing that everybody says, 'I can't imagine what you feel like,' and I say, 'You are absolutely right.' Because God does not give you that. He won't give you that, until you lose a child."

The family closed its doors to grieve. Only Georganna Traylor, Adrianne's aunt, put her nose out the door long enough to say, "We're so bitter and so hurt right now. I'm trying to keep pretty much sane over this."

6

RUMORS

The whispers around Mansfield High began early; first about Adrianne Jones's disappearance, then about a dead body.

There were 2000 students in the sprawling regional school on Walnut Creek Drive and, though there was no intercom announcement, by that afternoon a wave swept through the halls of the building that was so powerful, it was something measurable on the Richter scale. Desk drawers banged shut. Pencils were hurled. Fists slammed into walls. Stunned students gathered around lockers, outside classrooms, in the parking lot and the gym, on the soccer field, in the trailers that served as makeshift classrooms out back—the same places Adrianne Jones had been standing just two days before. Those who knew her were seized by an instant despair.

For many, instinctively and innately invincible, this was their first experience with death. Jeff Lackey, a junior, walked outside and threw himself on the ground, to cry. "It tore me up bad," he said later. "She was the first person I ever cared about a lot."

Principal Jerry Kirby immediately called in counselors, set aside special rooms to meet with students, made a brief announcement about Adrianne's death and encouraged kids to talk about their feelings.

"Anytime something like this happens, the entire student body, whether they knew the person or not, it affects them," said Cathy Britton, a coach for Mansfield's soccer team, which Adrianne had played on the year before.

Gary Foster's son was bombarded with questions. "We could never figure out how they knew where the body had been found," recalled Vickie Foster. "Most of the reporters never did get the location right. But all the kids seemed to know."

Jeff Lackey drove to the murder site. Over the next year dozens of kids would make the pilgrimage to the spot on Gary Foster's ground that marked the last resting spot for Adrianne Jones. But that day, the death was still fresh.

"You could almost see an outline of her body in the grass," Lackey recalled. "The grass was just soaked in a crimson color." The teenager made a cross out of two sticks and strands of red electrical tape and attached it to the barbed-wire fence that Adrianne had become tangled in as she fell dying.

Just up the hill, Gary Foster was too scared to sleep. "My first concern," he recalled, "was 'What if the killers think that we saw something?' We're out here in the middle of nowhere. If anybody wanted revenge, they could come out and there's nothing to stop 'em."

Foster went over the possibilities in his mind. "I

was thinking it was a drug problem. And if that's the case, they have no concern for human life. Plus, anyone who would kill one person could easily kill half-a-dozen more without thinking about it."

Those thoughts could easily get the heartbeat up. And, for days after the murder, the Foster family seemed to live on the verge of cardiac arrest. Their country home no longer seemed so pastoral; the quiet was killing them. Each time a car passed—or pulled off the road at the site of the murder—the Fosters jumped. "Gary didn't really sleep or eat for two weeks," recalled Vickie. "And I was scared to death. He'd usually get home from work before I would, but it would be dark when I got home. And just from the car to the house—you just got the feeling somebody's watching you. So he'd come out and stand there while I walked to the house. And we kept the gate closed."

Foster had guns in the house, but he was smart enough to know his limitations. "They're never handy," he said. "And if something happened, I'm sure I'd be too shocked to think where we had 'em or how to get to 'em."

But while the Fosters worried in the shadows of Seeton Road, people all over Mansfield were scared.

"Parents fear for their children," reported the *Mansfield News-Mirror.*

A Grand Prairie police investigator, quoted in the local paper, suggested that Adrianne may have been grabbed while jogging, which she liked to do "at odd hours when having difficulty sleeping." But by whom?

Police tried to calm fears about what kind of maniac might be lurking in the shadows of Main Street, but knew that not much would work except an arrest. "We don't have information that indicates any danger to other children at this point," an investigator responded. But he didn't have any information that warranted a feeling of security either.

There was also a story—helped by Adrianne's fun-loving reputation—that she had been killed at an all-night "rave" party near Denton, an hour's drive to the north, and dumped in Grand Prairie.

Many thought that drugs were involved—though no one knew if Adrianne did drugs.

Some suspected "Trisha," the girl who had attacked Kristin Clark with a bat and shot her boyfriend the year before. She had been heard to threaten Adrianne Jones after Adrianne testified against her in a court proceeding to keep her out of school.

Another story had it that a friend of Adrianne's had her killed because Adrianne had reported to her mother that she had gotten drunk at a party.

"About the only thing we didn't hear," Bill Jones would later say, "was that Adrianne had been abducted by aliens."

"Everyone was talking about it," recalled schoolmate Mary Bethune.

Everyone except David Graham. While most of Adrianne's friends seemed to feel the need be together and talk, Graham withdrew. "He just sat there," recalled one classmate. "He didn't really say anything. He listened to what everybody had to

say." They assumed that David was hurting like
they were, but wanted to be left alone.

Some of her friends were frightened.

"Those of us who were really close to Adrianne
were scared because we thought she might have
been killed because of something she knew," said
April Grossman, a classmate. "And we thought,
'Well, will the killer come after us, thinking that
Adrianne had told us the secret?' "

Who didn't have a secret? There were plenty of
secrets at Mansfield—and odd kids, violent ones
too. And there were plenty of guns.

"A lot of us had this weird feeling that the killer
was walking the halls with us," recalled April
Grossman.

7

DAVID AND DIANE

That Tuesday evening, the day after the body was found, David Graham put on his Civil Air Patrol uniform and drove the eight, nearly straight and flat, miles along Route 1187 west to the control tower building at the old Spinks Airport. He hadn't been to a C.A.P. meeting for a while—and didn't really want to go to this one. But he needed to see Diane. And they needed to be seen together.

Graham punched the numbers at the locked gate—1-1-8-7, just like the road number—and drove onto the airport grounds. Except for the Civil Air Patrol meetings and some occasional government agents flying in, the place was largely abandoned; all commercial traffic had moved into new quarters less than a mile south. This was perfect for C.A.P.—acres of old hangars for indoor marching and para-rescue training, as well as flight training, parties and cookouts.

Here in the north Texas plains, they were always on standby for tornado search-and-rescue duty, half the thrill of being part of the Civil Air Patrol. Before his pickup was totaled by Diane, Graham would stick blue flashing lights on top of his truck, pick up Green and Uekusa and then slog through rain and hail in search of people to save or property to rescue. During one storm the previous year, C.A.P. cadets had camped out at Spinks for nearly two days helping out in the aftermath of a storm.

Graham parked his secondhand station wagon near an old barracks building and marched quickly into the squat brick edifice with a round tower in the middle. Nothing was much the same for him anymore.

He had told Diane about Adrianne and all hell had broken loose. Now there was just this frantic feeling as he tried to make sense of what happened, moving on automatic pilot.

Normally, one of the adult officers would have called the meeting to order, briefed the group of uniformed teenagers about the evening's schedule, then turned to Graham with a crisp command, "Colonel Graham, take charge of the cadets."

And, just as normally, David Graham would have stood, twirled on one foot and faced the group confidently, saying, "Room, ten-hut!"

He would then have ticked off a list of announcements before dismissing the cadets to their various duties within the building, where they would spend the next several hours doing everything from attending aerospace seminars to monitoring the communications station to listening to visiting senior government agents share with their serious young charges information about counternarcotics missions down in South America.

This is what he had trained for all his life. He had kept the dream alive since the first grade, when his father took him to an air show in Brownsville and he decided he wanted to fly.

Afterward he wrote a letter to the Air Force to say he wanted to one day go to the Air Force Academy. His parents kept that letter, as well as dozens of elaborate drawings of airplanes, created out of his imagination, that David drew as a boy.

And, as soon as he turned thirteen, David got his mother to drive him to Spinks Airport to sign up for the South Fort Worth Composite Squadron, charter number 42154, of the Civil Air Patrol. Founded as a civilian patrol during World War II, it was one of the country's oldest and largest civilian military organizations sanctioned by the Defense Department. And its youth program, which dated to 1944, promised kids a rich and real military training experience.

During weekly meetings at Spinks, overseen by older teenage officers and supervising adults, young Graham flourished. He wore starched and pressed uniforms, stood at attention, marched in formation, studied text books about aeronautical engineering and slogged through mud on training exercises.

Graham memorized the C.A.P. motto—Semper Vigilans (Always Vigilant)—and the Cadet Oath:

I pledge that I will serve faithfully in the Civil Air Patrol Cadet Program, and that I will attend meetings regularly, participate actively in unit activities, obey my supervisors, wear my uniform properly and advance my training rapidly to prepare myself to be of service to my community, state and nation.

And he learned "The definition of military discipline":

Military discipline is that mental attitude and state of training which renders obedience instinctive under all conditions. It is founded upon respect for and loyalty to the properly constituted authority.

At some later period, "loyalty" would become a life-and-death issue in David Graham's life. And the big question would be whether anyone had taught him how to recognize "properly constituted authority." But for now, during these early years, David succeeded masterfully.

He fulfilled every part of his childhood dream, getting a pilot's license at age 14, learning how to be a leader, "wear rank," give orders. He aced his aerospace exam, easily ran the mile in less than the required time, attended moral leadership classes, loved survival-training courses,

David Graham was the quintessential all-American boy. At Mansfield High he also joined the Junior Reserve Officers' Training Corps, the Army's version of the Civil Air Patrol. He was as committed to ROTC as he was to C.A.P.

And he studied—or at least, he got excellent

grades. Some classmates thought he managed through osmosis.

"He could fall asleep during class and then wake up and still answer the teacher's questions," said classmate David Brennan.

"He didn't do his work, but he still had the highest average in the class," remembered a student who shared a French class with Graham his junior year.

The few girls who joined ROTC loved Graham because he stuck up for them. "He wouldn't let just anyone boss us around," recalled Joanna Christenson, who was in ROTC, a year behind Graham. "He was the most caring and respectful and respected person that I've ever met," said Sarah Layton, another ROTC cadet.

Layton, who was one of the few girls in the Junior ROTC program, recalled Graham coming to the girls' defense when they were being badgered by older boys. And he consoled one of the girls when her brother committed suicide.

He progressed so quickly up the ladder—Airman, Lieutenant, Captain, Cadet Colonel—that he became one of the most decorated cadet officers in the national history of the Civil Air Patrol. And he was slated to receive the Carl A. Spaatz Award, the highest cadet honor in the Civil Air Patrol.

But not tonight. Knots of cadets stood around somberly talking about the murder in Mansfield when David walked in. Since it was the first meeting of the month, they all wore their dress blues.

The color seemed appropriate to the mood. A half dozen of the teenagers were from Mansfield and knew Adrianne Jones. They spoke in hushed tones.

"Everybody was talking about what happened," recalled Jay Green, who attended nearby Burleson High and didn't know the victim. "But when I heard that she was shot, the first thing I thought was that it was a gang-related activity."

Green had been doing volunteer work with the "weed and seed" unit of the Fort Worth police department. And one thing he was learning was that drugs and gangs went together like drugs and murder.

He knew that Graham, if he showed up, would probably know the dead girl. Airman Radkey, who also went to Mansfield High, was trying to tell Green what happened, but was too shook up to talk.

"I knew her," she said, then started crying.

Just then Green looked up and saw Graham pushing through the glass doors. Everyone looked up. It was the first time many of them had seen Graham since he was relieved of his command. He hadn't even noticed that Zamora had arrived.

"But Graham just walked through," recalled Green, "tagged Zamora, and I didn't see them the rest of the night."

Things were different ever since Diane and David became an item. Zamora, one of the few girls in the South Fort Worth C.A.P. squadron, after a rocky start, had herself risen nicely through the ranks. Then she had completely fallen for Graham. No one could explain exactly how it happened, since they had known each other for nearly two years before falling in love. She seemed to contribute to his undoing—senior C.A.P. officers warned David that his attention to Zamora would undermine his career—though outside of C.A.P., it seemed a perfect match.

Only a few months younger than Graham, Zamora, a senior at nearby Crowley High School, seemed as determined and ambitious as he. At age nine, a year after the nation's schoolchildren watched the space shuttle Challenger explode, killing teacher Christa McAuliffe and six astronauts, Diane announced to her family that she wanted to be an astronaut. She sent away to NASA for brochures about the space program and found out that attending the Air Force Academy was one of the surest ways of getting into space.

It was several years later before she heard, over her middle school's public address system, an announcement about the Civil Air Patrol. It was the closest thing to astronaut training there was for a 13-year-old kid in Fort Worth.

To members of Diane's extended family, she was the bright star of the next generation. She would often be seen in church, poring over a school book instead of a prayer book.

"She was such a dedicated little girl," recalled her aunt Mary Mendoza. "I was always excited for her and the plans she had for her future. I remember times when I looked at her and wished I had been as smart and resourceful as she was when I was younger. When I learned that she was in Civil Air Patrol, I was very excited for her because she was doing something I'd always wanted to do. I always wanted to learn to fly. She would talk about becoming an astronaut and how one day she was going to the moon. In fact, she told me one time, 'I'm going to go beyond the moon.' ''

Some of her family wondered whether she was taking on too much by joining the Civil Air Patrol. She was already acting as a part-time mom for her younger sister and brothers while her mother got her nursing license. ''We didn't know how she was going to accomplish all that,'' recalled Sylvia Gonzalez, another aunt, ''but she was determined.''

''I went into it thinking it was going to be like Girl Scouts,'' recalled Zamora, ''but it wasn't.''

As it turned out, the Civil Air Patrol had more in common with the Green Berets than with the Girl Scouts. And Diane, who still kept teddy bears on her bed and was as independent-minded as she was disciplined, was not excited by taking orders or marching through the mud.

At C.A.P. meetings, she was often belligerent and seemed to bristle under the rules of strict hierarchy, including the orders of David Graham. One evening an exasperated officer shouted at her, ''Why do you even come if you won't follow orders?''

Zamora looked up calmly. ''I want to be in the Air Force,'' she replied. ''And I heard this is a good way to get in.''

David Graham helped change all that, proving, if

nothing else, that he was a good leader.

Under his direction, Zamora began to take her duties more seriously. He even convinced her to attend what was called Type A camp, which Diane once described as "a boot camp where you wake up with somebody yelling in your face and you're out marching at 6 A.M." She slogged through mud and pitched tent in the wild and ate MREs, the same "meals ready to eat" that soldiers scarfed down on the field of battle. "At first they're pretty nasty," she recalled, "but after a while you get used to it, and they're actually pretty good."

She did it because David Graham urged her on, she would say. And no one seemed to notice that the relationship had evolved into something more than an official military one—until the night Green noticed Diane nuzzling David Graham.

It was a hot summer evening. The fans were blowing through a briefing room crowded with sweating cadets sitting at desks in their dress blues. Graham stood in the front of the room, near a table with a radio, some models of rockets and manuals about rocket trajectory, leading a briefing about C.A.P. dues. Suddenly, he made eye contact with Flight Sergeant Zamora, who was sitting in the front row.

Then he went over to Zamora, leaned close to her and whispered something. She laughed. He laughed. Jay Green, who watched, was incredulous.

But as the night progressed, Green realized that something had happened between Graham and Zamora. They spent much of that evening together, talking, standing close, laughing. Other cadets also noticed the pair. No one said anything, but everyone knew what was at stake. It was a violation of the fraternization rules of the military; senior officers were never supposed to romance their juniors. It ruined discipline. It was bad for morale.

It was bad for Green's morale. That evening, after the meeting, he and Uekusa rode in the back of Graham's pickup for the first time. Zamora was in the cab. Their friend and leader had thrown them over for a girl.

Worse, Uekusa told Green later that night, "It's so unprofessional, so stupid," he said. "I can't believe he's doing this. He's ruining everything."

Though many others would comment about how similar David and Diane were, Green and Uekusa saw the two as very different. Graham was camouflage and combat boots, Zamora was teddy bears and lipstick; Graham hunted, Zamora talked. Graham was a guy, Zamora a girl.

Graham laughed at his friends. And Green and Uekusa got used to riding in the back of the truck, suffering the wind whizzing by their big naked ears while Graham and Zamora huddled together in the cab. At Brahms, Graham told his buddies to go ahead and get started; often they ate by themselves while Graham and Zamora smooched in the parking lot.

Though from very different backgrounds, the two high-achievers shared a self-discipline that won them honors and respect. They also shared an urge to join the military. And though they had known each other for nearly three years before dating, once it clicked, they seemed tó fall into each other's arms with an abandon that belied their drive.

At first the two enjoyed each other at the Friday night football games, cruised nearby Hulen Mall with friends or went to the parties at nearby Joe Pool Lake, since the warm days of summer lingered, in this part of Texas, well into fall.

They even shared a kind of solitude, an aloofness, about the world. Neither was a party animal; they didn't hang out in the Winn-Dixie parking lot on weekend nights—David worked at the Winn-Dixie as a "courtesy clerk." Their "crowds" were not large or boisterous. They weren't "joiners" except to further their ambition, an ambition that seemed focused on discipline and order. They always seemed older than their peers.

It wasn't long before David and Diane were spending all their free time together. And, as they grew more entwined, they began skipping social events, like track team cookouts or family gatherings. They even started skipping their Civil Air Patrol meetings, to go drinking together.

And when she showed up at her grandfather's church with a crew-cut young gringo in camouflage pants and combat boots, Diane's relatives couldn't believe it. "We were kind of surprised because Diane had never had a serious boyfriend," recalled one of her mother's sisters, Sylvia Gonzalez.

Diane was so studious she never had time for boys.

"She was always such a self-motivated child,"

said Gonzalez. "She knew exactly where she was going and what she wanted to be—an astronaut."

"She kept a spiral notebook with a list of what she had to accomplish in order to get a college scholarship," wrote Skip Hollandsworth in *Texas Monthly*. "She knew exactly what her grade point average and SAT scores needed to be. She carried a knapsack full of schoolbooks everywhere in case she got stranded and had some time to fill."

"Diane was always very serious about school and her studies," recalled Maggie Santos. "I rarely saw her when she didn't have that big bag that she carried all her school books in. She took it everywhere—even church—and was always reading or doing homework."

"She was a very hard worker, very motivated," recalled Betty Johnson, who was Diane's academic counselor through four years of high school. "Academics were her top priority and she worked really hard to reach her goal, which was to be admitted to the Air Force Academy."

"Her main goal and intent was to keep her academic standards high in order to get into the Academy," agreed track coach Linda Arnold.

"The thing Diane was most serious about was her studies," recalled family friend Mike Santos. "She talked about wanting to be an astronaut one day and it was very important to her that she be an honor student if she was ever to reach her goal."

"The Zamoras always held her up as an example to their other kids," recalled Maggie Santos. "And

I think that's one of the reasons Charles [a younger brother] and Jennifer [younger sister] are both honor students today. They had a good example in their older sister.''

"She talked a lot about her future," recalled Mike Santos. "She always seemed very mature for her age."

"She always had a smile for you—one of those shy-type smiles," recalled Lorena Jordan, a neighbor. "She was always so eager to please. You asked her to do something, she just always wanted to do it and do it well."

But she also had time for others. Lorena Jordan recalled that Diane made it a point when she was a senior to stop her son, Dane, then a freshman, in the hall at school and ask how he was doing.

Diane excelled in school and was active in academic-oriented clubs. She joined the Girl Scouts, took tap dance lessons. And, as a sixth-grader she tutored second- and third-grade children in math and English.

"She did all the young girl things and enjoyed them," recalled her aunt Sylvia.

Her mother called her "the disciplined one" of the family because she would start studying at six in the morning, before school.

It showed. She was a member of the student council, the Key Club, the National Honor Society and the Masters of the Universe, a science organization. She played flute in the marching band and ran on the cross-country team.

But her single-minded pursuit of well-roundedness was driven by her overriding desire to join the Air Force. At the end of her junior year, she asked that she be allowed to pose for her senior graduation picture wearing the special tassel marking her as part of the top 10 percent of the class. Though the request was a bit odd—given that it was premature—Diane said she wanted the picture as a way to keep her motivated.

But she rarely dated. And, despite her achievements, she was known as a quiet person. "She kind of kept to herself," Danny Webb, a Crowley junior, said of Zamora. "She had plenty of friends, though. She wasn't hard to talk to. She was just quiet."

Her aunt Martha Kibler described Diane as "carefree, always friendly, always studying, always very smart. In school, she liked to hang out with the smart kids rather than the 'in' crowd. She was never a part of the 'in' crowd."

"Diane was very quiet and reserved," said Linda Arnold, who coached Zamora on the junior varsity track team. "She kept to herself."

"She had her little circle of friends," said Charlie Painter, a Zamora classmate. And that circle kept to itself.

"She didn't really associate with many people," recalled Shane Johnson, a classmate.

A boy she dated her sophomore year recalled Diane asking to be taken home at 8:30 Valentine's night so she could study.

"She had this goal and she was going to achieve this goal no matter what," said Sylvia Gonzalez.

''She didn't have a lot of time for friends. Not even boyfriends. She never even thought about marriage or sex or having babies.'' Or so it seemed.

This was the summer that David's mother left and Diane confronted her father's mistress. Diane and David needed each other in more ways than one.

Janice Graham was the tightly wound mover-and-shaker of the family; her husband, a tall and gentle man, was the passive and pleasant former grade school principal. No one seemed to know why Jerry gave up being a principal to become a driving instructor for Sears; or why Janice seemed so intent on starting a flower and catering business.

There were suspicions of domestic disarray, but closed curtains in Mansfield were an iron veil. And no one dared to part it.

In fact, when Janice Graham took a job as a part-time art teacher at Mary Orr Intermediate School in 1993, she was planning independence from Jerry Graham.

Two years later, at the beginning of David's senior year, she took David's cross-country coach, Lee Ann Burke, aside and confided that she was separating from her husband.

''She told me to call if he wasn't handling things well,'' Burke recalled. ''She said, 'I don't want David to stop running on the team. I don't want his grades to suffer. Let me know if he's not eating or he's not doing well.' ''

It was Janice who moved out. But what surprised

many people who had known her was that she left her son. She had home-schooled her bright young boy in his early school years, encouraged him to excel at math and science and loyally drove him to his C.A.P. meetings. It was Janice, the parent with an especially tight bond with her son, who left home. David stayed with his father, in the little white clapboard house on Cedar Street. He was 17 and his father, now in his mid-sixties, was anything but a vigilant taskmaster.

David didn't talk about the separation. This was the summer he went to Canada, met Helen, fell in love with Diane, got engaged.

And he was soon to learn that Diane too had problems at home.

Diane's family had struggled economically from the time that she was born, January 21, 1977, the first of four children of Charles (Carlos) and Gloria Zamora.

Her father had just bounced a check at Dillard department store and there was a warrant for his arrest; when they caught up with him, police found that the new father had four outstanding speeding tickets on his record, a motor vehicle accident and a failure to appear in court. He finally settled the check-bouncing case, pleading guilty in 1979, and paid a $101 fine. At the time, he was 24 years old and his daughter, Diane, was 14 months old.

Carlos found some stability as an electrician at a small manufacturing company in Fort Worth and his wife, while working as a clerk at K mart on Cherry Lane, started going to nursing school. And by the time Diane was 12, she had three younger siblings and two working parents.

Diane "had to raise her brothers and sisters," said Sylvia Gonzalez, because both parents worked. "She had to grow up too fast. She was starved for love. She was always seeking attention. I told my sister this. I told her that she needed to spend more time with her children."

The Zamoras were buoyed by Gloria's family, especially the church that her father, Mike Mendoza, ran. The small, Spanish-speaking evangelical church in east Fort Worth was the center of family life. It was called Templo Juan 3:16, after Jesus's famous remark to the Pharisee Nicodemus: "For God so loved the world that he gave his only Son, that whoever believes in him should not perish but have eternal life."

And it was, as writer Tim Madigan described it, "a happy, friendly place where charismatic services were conducted in Spanish by Pastor Mike Mendoza, described as a godly man and inspiring preacher."

The small brick church on East Berry Street, painted a glistening and pure white, had no steeple or belltower, no statues or stained glass windows as did the majestic Travis Avenue Baptist Church just up the street. Nor was there any grandiose driveway at Templo Juan, as there was at Travis, with the Lexuses and Lincolns dropping off their Sunday charges. Beat-up vans and older model sedans pulled into the graveled parking lot of Templo Juan—passing Pastor Mike's silver Mercedes. The squat church sat on the leading edge of a poor Hispanic barrio, with big broad-leafed trees sheltering the cracking sidewalks, vacant lots littered with paper and old bicycles, and signs pounded haphazardly into dry grass reading "Se Venue" (for sale). On the church's northern side was a busy, four-lane commercial road. This part of East Berry was a no-man's-land of fast-food joints and used-car dealers, between the acres of black poverty in East Fort Worth and downtown, intersected, just a half-mile away, by a roaring interstate highway. There was a pawn shop—"fast cash jewelry and loans"—a gas station, a 7–11 and the Aquarium Tropical Fish Pet Shop across the street. And so it was in keeping with the neighborhood that the side of the white church would look like a billboard to drivers heading west on Berry: "Bienvenidos Templo Juan 3:16" in two-foot-high letters. "Un Oasis de Amor. Tel. 927–0379. Pastor Mike A. Mendoza."

The west wall of the church was higher and whiter and drivers heading east could see, just after passing McDonald's, "Jesus Is Lord" in tall, bright-red letters.

Diane sang in the church choir and studied the Bible with a group of young people called the "Missionettes." Her father played saxophone. The family, including some of Gloria's sisters and their families, met for services on Wednesday nights and Sunday mornings. Often after Sunday services, the various Zamora families would eat at a nearby cafeteria.

But just as the church was the Zamora family's

heart, it also seemed to be its undoing. It was in church one day in 1991 that Carlos Zamora met Connie Guel.

Then trying to cope with an abusive husband, Connie had come to church with her mother and left with a crush on the handsome man who played the saxophone in the choir. Not long after they met in church, Connie and Carlos became intimate. They managed to keep their affair a secret until one of Gloria's relatives saw the two in a grocery store. The entanglement then became a family affair, as Gloria and Carlos fought and Diane, the eldest, listened. Gloria Zamora often shared her frustrations with her oldest daughter. Guel recalled once listening from behind the closed bedroom door as Diane, who had come home early from school, rebuked her father for his infidelity. Guel left by way of the bedroom window rather than confront the outraged teenager.

At least twice over the next several years, Carlos Zamora moved out of his house and moved in with Guel. He was always back within a couple of weeks, swearing allegiance to his wife and family.

But the torrid affair continued and so did the family's financial troubles. Carlos slid from mid-level management to unemployment while maintaining his affair. Gloria pursued a nursing degree and sold Mary Kay cosmetics on the side. These were the years when Carlos, except for occasional odd jobs, was always out of work. He sometimes told his wife that he was going to work, but instead passed the day with his paramour.

The family lost two houses and filed for bankruptcy four different times in the course of six years.

At the eye of this domestic storm, young Diane took on even more responsibilities—caring for her younger siblings, trying to arbitrate between her parents, keeping her wits during frequent moves and, somehow, keeping her grades at honor student levels. There were nights when Diane studied by candlelight and flashlight because her parents hadn't paid the electric bill.

"She seemed to be the calming influence in her family," recalled neighbor Lorena Jordan. "When her mother would get upset or frustrated over something, it would be Diane who would say something like, 'Oh, Mom, everything's okay.' "

But as the domestic turmoil grew more heated, Diane's role also became more complicated.

On several occasions the affair seemed to consume the whole family, as Carlos and Gloria and Connie argued with the children looking on. Once, at the end of April 1995, as Diane finished her junior year at Crowley High, she accompanied her mother on a mission to confront Connie and Carlos. But when they arrived on Guel's block and saw her car, they mistakenly stormed the house that the car was parked in front of. "An old man lived in the house," Guel recalled. "He had just gotten home from the hospital and was in bed when the two women barged in and started ransacking everything."

According to the police report, after scattering papers and mail around, Diane and Gloria realized their mistake and left. They went through Guel's car, which was unlocked, and took, according to the complaint that Guel filed, Carlos's gold Seiko watch, a pair of his sunglasses and the pawn ticket for his beloved saxophone. Over the next month a series of phone calls from Gloria provoked Connie into filing a harassment suit against her. She charged that Gloria would threaten, "Wait and see what happens to you next."

The next day Gloria filed her own charges against Connie, complaining that her husband's mistress called her and gave "explicit details" of what she and Carlos did together.

Despite this chaos—or perhaps because of it—Diane made herself the most disciplined and moral of beings.

It was in the middle of all of this, at the end of the summer of 1995, that Diane announced to her family that she was dating David Graham, a boy from Civil Air Patrol and that it was serious. All anyone knew was that the two of them fell madly in love. And their lives, as friends and family had previously known them, changed.

"We're a large family," recalled Sylvia Gonzalez. "Every Sunday, we'd go to church and then go eat afterward. The whole family. Children, too. Diane was very much a part of that until David came into the picture. . . . But once he came along, she was totally wrapped up in him. . . . She thought he hung the moon."

"This was more than an infatuation," recalled Linda Arnold. "It was very intense. They were each other's best friend."

"It seemed like after they started dating, I never

saw Diane without him except for when she missed the bus and I gave her a ride to school," recalled Lorena Jordan. "Otherwise, they were always together when I saw them.

"She used to stop by the house all the time, just to say hello. But after she started seeing David, we didn't see her that much. I remember that I had a hard time getting her graduation gift to her. Finally, she came by one afternoon—with David—to pick it up. . . .

The first time I ever met him was one day when I was babysitting Jennifer and he appeared at the front door. He didn't even bother to identify himself, just saying he wanted to take Jennifer. I asked who he was and he wouldn't say. Finally, after I told him I wasn't going to let her go, he said, 'Well, Diane's sitting in the car.' I went out and told Diane that she should have come to the door. I didn't appreciate the way he acted."

"When David came along it was like they were obsessed with each other," said Sylvia Gonzalez. "He had to be at every family function. You couldn't get physically close to her or he would be there, between you."

David talked about Diane at school, even showed pictures of her to friends. "They were both madly in love with one another," recalled Kevin Crawford, a Mansfield high schoolmate who double-dated with Graham and Zamora.

Once David bought Diane a pair of $100 combat boots because her family couldn't afford them. He called her Kittens and she called him Tiger. And they invented their own odd farewell, "Greenish brown female sheep," a bit of wordplay meant to mean "I love" (greenish brown is olive—I love); "you" (ewe, the female sheep). Olive ewe. I love you.

David got Diane to listen to Pearl Jam and Diane got David to quit White Zombie. Christian music was thrown over for hard rock. And necking became sex.

"She kept telling us she wanted to focus on her studies and her goals instead of on guys," recalled Sylvia Gonzalez. "And she always made it a point to tell us she was never going to lose her virginity unless she got married. When two of her cousins got pregnant in high school, she said she couldn't believe how stupid they were. She swore that nothing like that would happen to her."

Diane had dumped a sophomore-year boyfriend when she decided he only wanted to have sex with her.

"She always wanted to wait until she was married," said a former date. "That was one of the main morals she had."

Then came David and it all went out the window—including virginity. Diane told David on many occasions about her need to wait until she married. He pressed, but she was adamant. As their love increased, however, Diane's resolve melted. "Diane had always held her virginity as one of her highest virtues," recalled David. "When we agreed to be married she finally let her guard down long enough for our teenage hormones to kick in."

Diane immediately doubted what she had done. She told her mother what had happened. "She was real confused," said one of her relatives. "I know she felt guilty because she had wanted to wait. But once she went through with it, she became more committed than ever to David. I remember her saying, 'If I can't be Mrs. David Graham, then I will die as Miss Diane Zamora.'"

Graham's C.A.P. buddies watched in mild astonishment as their old friend let his hair grow and his shirt hang out, started wearing gaudy rings on his fingers and then—it seemed so quick, but so predictable—announce his wedding plans.

He even made it part of his "current event" talk in his ROTC class. "My current event is I'm engaged," he said. "I'm getting married after I graduate from the Air Force."

Not surprisingly, at least for this determined and disciplined couple, David and Diane set a date—it was five years away, August 13, 2000, as soon as they graduated from their respective academies—though they had yet to be officially accepted.

"They were going to charter a bus to carry their relatives in Texas to the famous Cadet Chapel on the Air Force Academy campus," wrote Skip Hollandsworth in *Texas Monthly*. "There, David would wear his uniform, Diane a white wedding dress, and at the end of the ceremony, they would walk under crossed swords held by other cadets."

It sounded like a movie-scenario wedding.

Then, on a dark evening in late September, Diane, driving David's truck home alone, lost control on a back road—and nearly lost her life when the pickup flipped over several times. She had her left arm outside the cab and the truck landed on it. Rushed to the hospital, doctors had to reattach the skin that had been peeled back from three of her fingers; for a time they thought they might have to amputate.

David hurried to the hospital and was at Diane's bedside every night while she recuperated. "Unlike that other boyfriend of hers who just wanted to go all the way," said one relative, "David genuinely cared for Diane. I don't think Diane had ever had that kind of attention."

For some of her relatives, this was the first time they met the new love interest they had all heard about—and they were in for an additional shock. "I visited her in the hospital and met David for the first time," recalled Martha Kibler, one of Diane's aunts. "Diane introduced me to him as her fiancé then."

Diane's aunt Mary Mendoza, who lived in Austin, also visited her niece at the hospital. "I knew she had a boyfriend," recalled Mendoza, "but I hadn't met him at that point. When I visited her in the hospital and she told me she was engaged, I was shocked. I asked who David Graham was and she explained that they had met in Civil Air Patrol. My first reaction was that I thought it was pretty neat; that they had the same interests and all.

"What surprised me was that Diane had always

said she was never getting married,'' said Mendoza. ''She said she didn't even like boys. I'm pretty sure she had never had a real boyfriend before she met David Graham.''

Others remembered Diane not being interested in marriage at all. ''We used to go out for dinner—us and our three kids, the Zamoras and their four,'' recalled Mike Santos, ''and Diane would get embarrassed if the younger ones started acting up. It tickled me and I'd tell her, 'Just wait until you get married and have kids of your own.' She said she was never going to get married.''

And the feeling of empathy for having found someone special, was mixed with worry about whether the couple was really ready for marriage— even if it was almost five years off. ''Until she met David,'' recalled her Aunt Sylvia, ''she'd maybe had three dates.''

But after she got out of the hospital, David proved himself a loving and loyal fiancé. He drove Diane to rehabilitation sessions, bought her medicine, encouraged her to apply to the Naval Academy when it was clear that she would not be ready for the Air Force's physical exams. She could apply to the Naval Academy and still become an astronaut, he told her.

The scars on Diane's left hand would be visible for months after the accident. And she had limited movement of her fingers, which increased the difficulty of doing the required sit-ups and push-ups for her physical fitness exams. She had three different operations over the next three months to try to reconstruct her hand. At one point Diane thought she might lose her left ring finger to the accident.

Throughout the ordeal, David was loving and loyal.

They did homework together and worked on their military school applications together. He urged her to sign up for cross-country so she could pass the physical fitness tests to qualify for the Academy. David even hocked some of his beloved hunting rifles for a down-payment on an engagement ring, which Diane couldn't wear yet because of her auto injury.

Finally, it seemed, she had found the boyfriend who could help her stay motivated, who provided in love what she had sought through academics and who gave her the single-minded attention her parents weren't able to provide.

There would be no Colonel Graham taking charge this December night. It wasn't surprising. Graham's fall from military grace had been as swift and unexpected as his rise had been steady and anticipated.

The senior officers were still baffled by their award-winning cadet. They even debated whether to try to stop the machinery that was already printing out the Spaatz certificate. David had passed the academic and leadership tests, written his essay and met the physical muster necessary to receive the award before he began to dissolve. And he had earned a lot of points over the years and made the 42154 Squadron proud—fewer than one percent of all C.A.P. cadets in the country had earned the award over the 50-year history of the organization. Taking it away from him at this point would hurt everyone.

At the Civil Air Patrol meeting that night, talk of Graham's upcoming award was the only good news in the otherwise bleak evening.

But Graham and Zamora huddled most of the time in the warren of corridors and offices in the basement of the building—and left early. There was no offer of a ride to Green.

"He'll grow out of it and be a damn good pilot," Green recalled thinking. "He'll grow more common sense."

Instead, Graham had already made the worst mistake of his life. He had been heading in that direction. The piling-on of conflicting demands and passions—with no mother to guide or supervise—seemed to have pushed him to the edge of sanity, then to a vacant lot behind an old grade school. Having only just presented Diane with an engagement ring—and even more recently taken her precious virginity—David had been racked with guilt about his sexual liaison with Adrianne.

Diane recalled David showing up at her house that November night and seeming distracted. "He had this look in his eyes that was horrible," she recalled. "He looked so scared. He had this red stuffed-animal dog in his hands. I could tell something was wrong but I figured he was just tired."

David spent the night, but said nothing.

The next day, he told Jay Green in Burleson. But

by now, between his adventures in Canada, his shortlived long-distance romance with Helen and his hotter-than-lava affair with fellow cadet Zamora, whom Green didn't care for, Graham was losing Green's interest.

"We were busy doing something else at the time and I didn't pay much attention," Green recalled.

David seemed to drift more erratically, not realizing, in the heat of passion, how poisonous his sexual betrayal would be—made unexpectedly more noxious by Diane constantly reminding David how happy she was.

"I was always being told by Diane that our relationship was so perfect and pure," David would later say. "The love we shared would never be broken and no one would ever come between us."

Now that someone had broken through, what should be done? The corrosiveness of living the lie ate at David's discipline until, on November 21, 1995, he was relieved of his Civil Air Patrol command by adult officers and warned that his attentions to Zamora would undermine his career aspirations.

Later that week, David accompanied Diane to a Mendoza family Thanksgiving gathering. He seemed preoccupied. "He just nodded and said 'Hi' when Diane introduced us," recalled Mary Mendoza. "He seemed quite introverted."

Unable to focus, his Air Force dream going up in smoke, David could no longer hide. "[Diane] knew in my eyes that something was wrong," he recalled. But he couldn't have imagined what his confession would bring.

Diane recalled that night very vividly. They had just pulled up in front of Diane's house.

"I was questioning him about past relationships because he always told me that I was his first real girlfriend," Diane remembered.

Diane had always wondered about that statement since she knew that most of her contemporaries had some kind of relationship by the time they were seniors in high school. And she made him name all the girls he had known or gone places with.

"I will never forget him mentioning the name Adrianne," recalled Diane, "because that name kind of stuck in my head."

She now began peppering David with questions about Adrianne. "For some reason," she recalled, "I felt like I needed to ask about Adrianne."

But the more she pressed, the more David seemed to hesitate. When they reached an uncomfortable impasse, they decided to go in the house. David wanted to change the subject, and, for a moment, it seemed as if they had moved on.

"We got into a big fight," she said, "because, as always, he was trying to make me study for the SAT and I didn't want to." They argued for several more minutes about the test, but just as they seemed to have calmed themselves, David turned toward Diane.

"I have something to tell you that is really important," he said.

"I kind of knew that he was going to tell me,

just by the way he looked at me," recalled Diane.

"You haven't been the only girl in my life," David said. "I have had sex with someone else before."

Diane stared at him, in shock.

"You mean you weren't a virgin when we met?"

"No, I was."

But that made Diane feel even worse, since it meant that he had lost his virginity *after* they began dating.

"She knew in my eyes that something was wrong the moment I decided to confess," recalled David, "When I did tell her, I thought the very life in her had been torn away."

The life quickly returned, however—like a violent storm. Diane began sobbing, shaking, screaming. She grabbed a fireplace iron and swung it wildly at David.

But no sooner had Graham wrestled the brass bar from Diane than she threw herself wildly around the room. "I kept ramming my head against the walls," she remembered. "On the ground I kept ramming my head onto the floor and tried to crack my skull. I just didn't want to live with what he had said to me."

"For at least an hour she screamed sobs that I wouldn't have thought possible," David would later write in prose similar to Victorian tabloid. "It wasn't just jealousy. For Diane, she had been betrayed, deceived and forgotten all in that one meaningless instant in November. The purity which she held so dear had been tainted in that one unclean act.''

''I felt like I had lost everything,'' recalled Diane. ''My hand wasn't working the way it should, my family wasn't in the best financial state, and now he was telling me the one thing I prized more than anything else was taken away.''

''Diane didn't want Adrianne to be the same woman for me that her father had in his affair,'' David would later say.

Still banging her head on the floor, Diane screamed, ''Kill her, kill her.''

The stunned Graham tried to calm his fiancée. But nothing seemed to work until he said yes.

''The request of Adrianne's life was not for a second taken lightly by me,'' he would recall. But at the same time, he would think, ''I couldn't even believe she would ask that of me.''

But it seemed to be the only thing that calmed Diane. ''David promised that he would do that,'' recalled Diane, ''and David never has broken a promise to me before.''

At no other time did David and Diane's individual strengths combine so recklessly as now. The same passion that had driven Diane to overcome the disorder of her family now hurled her to a frenzied hatred of a girl she didn't even know, but whom she considered a rival. And the same meticulous and disciplined attention to goals that had made David a standout at Mansfield High now turned him toward a determined loyalty to Diane and a bizarre promise.

*   *   *

David analyzed the situation as he would have a military objective. And he reasoned his way right to the depths of hell.

"The only thing that could satisfy her womanly vengeance was the life of the one that had, for an instant, taken her place," David would later write, in stilted, emotionless prose, as if it made perfect sense. "Diane's beautiful eyes have always played the strings of my heart, effortlessly. I couldn't imagine life without her. Not for a second did I want to lose her. I didn't have any harsh feelings for Adrianne, but no one could stand between me and Diane. I was totally in love with her and always will be."

No, he couldn't believe that Diane would "demand" murder; but neither could he take her request "lightly."

Though Diane would recall what happened next as a kind of falling downstairs—"Nothing was really premeditated because I think we were both acting in passion"—David took Diane's murderous plea as an "ultimatum" and "thought long and hard about how to carry out the crime."

In the recalling of their thinking at the time, it seemed that each wanted *not* to go forward; but neither was capable of singlehandedly bringing the mad carousel to a stop.

They spent that weekend calling Adrianne. But she was never home. Diane became increasingly anxious, stressed between the bizarre thought of murder and the image of her fiancé having sex with another woman. "I would wake up in the middle of the night with nightmares," she recalled. "I couldn't even look at his face because I had thought he was a different person. I had horrible pictures running through my head about what happened between him and Adrianne and they made me feel really sick."

The sexual images and the passions they spawned were powerful and immediate; the homicidal thoughts, abstract. It was as if Diane's jealous rage fanned the flames of David's obsessional loyalties. Individually, harmless; together, David and Diane were a lethal liaison. She provided the ends; he, the means.

That Saturday and Sunday, when he wasn't calling Adrianne or trying to calm Diane, David thought about how to carry out the murder. But he didn't tell Diane what his plan was—he had always been the planner in their relationship, the leader—until after he had finally reached Adrianne on the phone. It was 10:30 Sunday evening. She told David she was on the other line, but that may have only made it easier for David to make the arrangements—to pick Adrianne up later that night. He would be there at 12:30, he told her, when she was sure that her parents would be asleep.

But the two young plotters hesitated. They were late leaving Diane's house. They let the 12:30 A.M. rendezvous pass. Adrianne must have been lying on her waterbed in the dark, still in her workout clothes, listening in the quiet for the car's engine outside.

At the appointed hour, David and Diane were driving Diane's parents' green Mazda up to the Grahams' small clapboard on Cedar Street. Perhaps it wouldn't happen. They went into his bedroom. It looked to Diane as if he "put together what he was going to do really quick," she recalled, because "he sat me down at his house for about five minutes to calm me down and throw stuff in his bag."

In fact, David had thought about it. They would pick Adrianne up, he explained to Diane, drive her to Joe Pool Lake and kill her there. "The plan was for David to break her neck and sink her body to the bottom of Joe Pool Lake," recalled Diane. While outlining the plan, David hurriedly put rope, barbells and his 9-mm Russian-made Makarov pistol in a duffel bag on the floor. They were all familiar items. As familiar as Diane seemed to be with rage, David was similarly at home with the grip of a gun.

It was past one o'clock when they found themselves—unexpectedly, perhaps—ready. It was as if the two teenagers were stalling for time, hoping, perhaps, for the fates to intervene or for time to break in on their dance.

"I think we expected to get caught really fast," Diane would say, "because we didn't spend much time thinking about what we were doing." Even at a point when David would have Adrianne grasped around the throat, the pair seems to pause, Diane saying, "I could kind of tell he didn't want to do anything."

But at every juncture, every point of hesitation,

continue they did, as if from a Poe formula, "Slowly I turned, step by step. . . ." It took less than ten minutes for David to drive down East Broad Street, by the Golden Fried Chicken where Adrianne worked, then down Walnut Creek Drive— less than a mile altogether—to the Joneses' modest ranch house.

Diane, as part of the plan, had slipped behind the rear seat of the hatchback as they wheeled through the dark and deserted town. Adrianne was waiting.

In separate interviews, nearly a year later, Diane and David would each recall that night in vivid, if only slightly different, detail.

> David: The plan was to call Adrianne and convince her to come out to my car. That worked.

> Diane: She came out to the car and got in. I was in the trunk and David was driving. I remember being real scared because at a time like that when you kind of know what's happening, you really don't trust anyone. I remember wanting to turn back.

> David: The plan was to drive her out near Joe Pool Lake. That worked.

A description of the ride to the lake, what was said or done during what must have been at least a 20-minute drive along narrow and dark country roads, is mysteriously missing from both Diane and David's accounts.

Diane: I was afraid to move so I just laid still in the trunk. David later told me that he felt the same way, that he wanted to turn back and take her home, but he was afraid of what I would do or say if he turned back.

David: The plan was to (and this is not easy for me to confess) break her young neck and sink her to the bottom of the lake with the weights that ended up being hit into her head. That didn't work.

Diane: David usually always has a gun of some sort with him all the time. I knew that he had the Makarov 9-millimeter with him. I also knew that he had the weights. I don't think we knew what we were really going to do. It was more like we were going to get out there and just do it. David never specified an exact location of where he was going because I don't think he even knew where he was going.

David: Diane was hidden in the back of the car.

Diane: David pulled over to the side of the road and Adrianne had already leaned her seat back and he started, I guess pretending, that he was going to kiss her, and he motioned for me to pull the hatch down. I remember getting out and seeing that and it made me all the more angry. I knew he didn't mean it, but it just made a bunch of pictures run in my head again. When she saw me she kind of freaked out. David held her down and said it's OK, we just want to talk to you. I think at that point I could kind of tell he didn't want to do anything. I asked Adrianne about she and David having sex and she said that she didn't enjoy it, that there was too much guilt. I guess it was the way she looked at me when she said it that made me so angry. Even now I can only remember her eyes, but not her face. I remember screaming at David all over again. All of it just became so real. I think I got kind of hysterical and I screamed, "Just do it. Just do it." David just started wrestling with her basically and she was trying to get away from him.

David: I realized too late that all those quick, painless snaps seen in the movies were just your usual Hollywood stunts. The quick and painless crime turned into something that basically scared the @#$% out of Diane and I.

Diane: I remember being scared that she was going to hurt him and so I reached to the back where I knew the weights were on the ground to try to hit her with it. I missed.

David: We realized that it was either her or us and Diane struck her in the back of the head with one of the weights while I held her.

Diane: I was just too nervous and my hands were just shaking too much. Probably the third time I did hit her on the head with the weight. Things kind of calmed down real quick and I was still really scared.

David: I could see in Diane's eyes that she was confused and scared. She was first acting out of passionate rage, but now she was fighting from instinct.

Diane: I think the whole time the only thing going through my mind was what was I doing, but I knew that things had gone too far and I couldn't stop. Somehow stopping seemed scarier than going on. David turned his back. I don't really remember why and she slipped out of the window and ran off.

David: Adrianne somehow crawled through the window and to our horror, ran off.

Diane: We started to follow her with the car but we didn't go far because she collapsed into a field on the side of the road. David jumped out of the car with his gun because he didn't want to leave someone there. They could say something against us. He started running after her but she collapsed before he got to her.

David: I was panicky and just grabbed the Makarov 9-millimeter to follow. To our relief (at the time) she was too injured from the head wounds to go far. She ran into a nearby field and collapsed. I wanted to just jump in and drive off.

Diane: He ran back to the car and he said, "She's dead." I was just too scared and I said, "Are you sure? No, she's not." I told him to shoot her. "She's not dead."

David: We were both shaken and even surprised by the nature of our actions. Neither Diane nor myself were ever violent people. In that short instant I knew I couldn't leave the key witness to our crime alive. I just pointed and shot.

Diane: He was really panicky and he wanted to take off, but he went back to where she was 'cause I told him to.

David: I was very confused and scared. I probably looked like the proverbial headless chicken running around the crime scene. I fired again and ran to the car.

Diane: He shot her twice in the head. He ran back and jumped into the car and drove off as quick as he could.

David: Diane and I drove off. The first things out of our mouths were, "I love you," followed by Diane's, "We shouldn't have done that, David." "Well, nice time to tell me." I just wanted it to be a dream.

Diane: I remember the first words out of his mouth were, "I love you, baby. Do you believe

me now?" I said, "Yes, I believe you, I love you
too." I said, "What have we done?" His reply
was, "I don't know. I can't believe we just did
that." We drove off. The whole time I was pretty
panicky. We both knew what we had done was
wrong and we both regretted it.

Some part of David and Diane had obviously not
wanted to go through with the killing. Unfortunately
for Adrianne Jones, the wrong part at the wrong
time was in charge; they didn't turn back. And now
they drove through the dark night all the way to
Burleson, knocking finally on Jay Green's window.

"I think we were afraid to look at each other,"
Diane later said, "and in some ways I think we
were really afraid of each other."

After washing up, desperately scrubbing at the
blood on David's clothes, they lay down on Green's
bedroom floor and tried to sleep. But it was impossible. Diane began shaking uncontrollably. "I broke
down crying," she recalled, "because I was so
scared, and we held each other and prayed that God
would forgive us for what we had done."

When they left Green, they drove to Diane's parents' house in Fort Worth, stopping a block away
to toss David's bloodied pants into a Dumpster.
They pulled into the garage of Zamora's Gatlinberg
Drive house. Now, for the first time, under the harsh
electric light, they could see Adrianne's blood in the
car. David jumped out gagging. Diane could see his
face was a ghastly white.

"He was really pale and sick to his stomach,"

recalled Diane. "He wouldn't even step back into that car for months because it was so horrible of a memory. So I cleaned it up while he was in the bedroom asleep. I told him just to go to sleep because he had gone into the bathroom to vomit. He said he was pretty sick to his stomach."

After she finished cleaning the car, Diane went to the bedroom where David was. "I told him to come sleep by the fire and so we both went out there and slept by the fire, the whole time thinking the police were going to come to the door and arrest us."

But there were no police. In fact, if there were the possibility of committing the perfect murder, they had inadvertently stumbled onto it.

"I told everybody all along," recalled Chuck Sager, who headed the police investigation, "any time more than one kid does a crime, we solve it. Period. One of them always talks. That's the name of the game. That's life. So either one kid did this and we've got a sick mind—or we're going to learn about it."

What the cops hadn't figured on was a fluke of geography. The other kid, Diane, lived 20 miles away, didn't know Adrianne or any of her friends. Even David's best friends, from the Civil Air Patrol, Joseph Uekusa and Jay Green, lived in a different town and didn't know Adrianne Jones. Though many Mansfield students knew that David and Adrianne were friends, she had many friends. No one knew about the sex—David had only told his Burleson friends, who didn't know Adrianne. As in a good terrorist network, David and Diane lived highly compartmentalized lives.

"They were able to stick together and keep their mouths shut," said Sager.

David's father called the Zamoras that morning to make sure his son was up and going to school.

But he had also relayed some shocking news. "Did you hear about that girl from Mansfield that was killed?" he asked his son.

David mumbled that he hadn't.

When he hung up, he told Diane. "Up to that point I don't think either of us really thought she was dead," recalled Diane.

8

REMEMBERING ADRIANNE

He didn't want to go, but there was David Graham standing in the back of First United Methodist Church on Pleasant Ridge Drive, hearing Adrianne's favorite song, Annie Lennox's "No More 'I Love You's'" being played and Bill and Linda Jones speaking.

As a member of the cross-country team, David was invited to a private memorial for Adrianne, whose body was cremated.

At that moment he wished he could turn back the clock. There were tears in his eyes.

He wanted Adrianne to be alive.

"I wanted to able to drive Adrianne back home," he thought, "to go to sleep and to wake up back on December 3 free to make decisions all over again."

He and Diane had it so good. They had helped each other through so much already. His parents breaking up, her parents breaking up. They had been there for each other. Now this. They would have to be with each other for this.

Holding back tears, Adrianne's father said, "You could not sculpture, construct, put together or de-

sign a nicer, neater, more intelligent, more dedicated, more independent or more beautiful child.''

On the altar was a framed photograph of Adri-
anne, the one taken just a few weeks before, that
Linda had planned on presenting to her daughter for
Christmas.

Linda Jones invited members of the soccer and
cross-country teams, the Fellowship of Christian
Athletes and the Mansfield High faculty, to remember her daughter ''for the good things she did.''

For the next week, Adrianne's murder was all
that anyone in Mansfield could talk about. ''Every
civic, social and religious meeting devoted a moment to silence or prayer on behalf of the slain
girl,'' reported the *News-Mirror*. Many people wore
ribbons in Adrianne's honor.

At a memorial tree planting at the high school's
soccer field, coach Cathy Britton, tears in her eyes,
remembered Adrianne as a smiling, pony-tailed girl
who loved romping across the field, getting dirty,
but always smiling. After Britton spoke, tears well-
ing in her eyes, students passed a shovel around,
taking turns digging a hole for a memorial tree.
Many were crying.

Linda Jones managed to stand in front of the
group, just days after her daughter was brutally
murdered, and speak. She asked everyone there, on
this sun-drenched December afternoon, to hold
hands. ''Unity,'' said Jones. ''There is unity of
numbers. Strength. We draw strength from that
unity. That gives us courage to face the evils in this
world.

"She's with each of you," Linda Jones told the group. "As the days and the weeks and the years go by, you'll remember Adrianne with happy memories."

Holding hands, the kids raised their voices together, "Unity! Strength! Courage!"

Some of Adrianne's friends began to make pilgrimages to the murder scene. Even Linda Jones ventured out to the site. But she went with Jeff Lackey and Jessica Ramon, after dark, to hunt for evidence. Police could not find a diamond stud earring and gold necklace that Linda was sure Adrianne had on the night she was murdered.

Lackey noticed that the cross he made was gone. He didn't know it at the time, but investigators had carefully removed the crude memorial and dusted it for fingerprints, believing it could have been put there by Adrianne's killer.

"Linda just felt like they missed something," recalled Ramon. "I remember being scared, and being cold and shaking because Jeff and I were blowing smoke and our noses were red. I felt really dumb, like we were crazy people looking through the weeds."

But Linda Jones, who would consult psychics to try to find out what had happened to Adrianne, wasn't concerned about looking crazy. Every day she wore a piece of Adrianne's clothing or dabbed on some of Adrianne's makeup; part memorial, part psychic investigation. The family left a light on in Adrianne's room, "as if hoping their daughter would find her way home," wrote journalist Skip

Hollandsworth. "Kids drove past the house, staring through the open curtains, able to see Adrianne's vanity, where she had put on her makeup, her stereo, and her bookcase that still held a couple of her Stephen King novels."

It would always be thus: the recognition of the reality and its denial would reside side-by-side for some time.

"We hardly ever got to see her," Linda Jones would later say. "She was always busy. You know that's how it's supposed to be, though. You grow up and become independent."

9

AN ARREST

The local *Mansfield News-Mirror* eulogized Adrianne Jones in a front-page story as "an exemplary honor student, diligent employee and competent athlete," a "well-rounded teenager." But, said the paper, her death "provokes more questions than answers."

The biggest question was: Who killed her?

A team of investigators, led by detectives from the Grand Prairie police department, set up a command post in the Mansfield police department and began working round the clock to solve the murder.

They made phone calls to police agencies and school officials, talked to friends, combed and recombed the murder site and staked out the school. The full-time team, headed by Detectives Dennis Clay and Dennis Meyer of Grand Prairie, came to include Detective Julie Bain of Mansfield and, from time to time, a member of the Texas Rangers. The death of a pretty teenager had made front-page news throughout the region and local politicians wanted the case solved.

"These guys came together and worked as a team

like I've never seen in my 23 years in law enforcement,'' recalled Sergeant Chuck Sager, the officer
in charge of the Grand Prairie Crimes Against Persons unit that would be investigating Joneses' murder.

It wasn't easy, since there were jurisdictional
jealousies to respect. Adrianne Jones lived in Mansfield, as did her family and most of her friends. Her
high school was in Mansfield. Some of Mansfield's
police knew the Joneses.

But the rivalries were put aside for Adrianne.
Grand Prairie cops came to appreciate Mansfield's
help. ''People tend to open up to one of their own,''
said Grand Prairie police officer Douglas Clancey.
A number of Mansfield police were assigned to the
case.

And Mansfield police knew that Grand Prairie,
with five times the number of officers on its force,
had much more experience in these things.

Sager had seen a lot in two decades. One of the
first cases he worked as a detective, in 1982, was
that of a disenchanted truck driver who had gone
around town shooting former bosses and colleagues,
killing six people in three different locations before
finally ramming a hijacked 18-wheeler into a road-
block.

Despite some outrageous crimes, however, Sager
remembered them as innocent days, when the lieutenant, the captain and the chief of police had to be
alerted every time there was a robbery, rape or murder. ''Now, nobody calls the chief on any of them,''

explained Sager. "And the lieutenant and deputy chief are called only on murders."

From a sleepy town of 50,000, Grand Prairie had become a sprawling suburb of over 100,000, eating up farmland and lapping at Mansfield's door. "We used to be wide open spaces down here 15 years ago," Sager recalled. "Now, this area is as dense as the east coast. There's 5 million people living in the Dallas–Fort Worth Metroplex."

And, along with having Great Adventure and the Cowboys close by, Mansfield also seemed to have been absorbed into the general mayhem of the metropolis. Earlier in the year a Mansfield man kidnapped his estranged wife after shooting her boyfriend to death.

A few months later Jennifer Yesconis was convicted of arranging the murder of her father and stepmother in their Mansfield home; the 20-year-old woman hoped to collect on a life insurance policy—early.

And many Mansfield residents were still talking about Steven Robards, a 38-year-old divorced man whose 1993 death was considered natural until Robards's teenage daughter, Marie, a transfer student to Mansfield High, confessed to a friend a year later. She had wanted to live with her mother in a different town, Marie told the classmate, and so had poisoned her father, by slipping barium acetate—stolen from a high-school chemistry class—into his take-out Mexican food. Marie Robards was awaiting trial.

"The violence over the last four or five years has scared me," said retired district judge Scott Moore.

"Young people don't have any appreciation for life, either their own or others'."

Some people theorized that the violence was a kind of copycatting; at least, an emotional virus that had taken hold. "When you see clustering in one area of the country," said criminologist Doctor Jack Levin of Northeastern University in Boston, "you have to think seriously of copycat influences. That's especially true among teenagers."

What seemed even more true of teenagers, however, was their ability to create work for the police by simply being teenagers.

Most of what police found in the early rounds of interviewing about Adrianne were reasons to dismiss theories about sour drug deals and all-night rave parties.

"Unlike an average adult, who may have a circle of twenty good friends, a high school kid may have a hundred or a hundred and fifty friends," recalled Sergeant Sager, "A high-school kid is in all these different classes each day and develops many different relationships."

And in the case of Adrianne Jones, a popular student who worked in a popular drive-in, the number and variety of relationships was even higher.

Though a reward fund set up by the Overton Bank and Trust, just down the street from Adrianne's house, had more than $10,000 in it, police were flooded with "leads" from teens who could have cared less about the money.

"Most kids don't have the level of responsibility or maturity that an adult has," recalled Sager. "So

the rumors really fly. In fact, they just make stuff
up. They think things are true because it passes in
front of their brain.''

They interviewed everyone on the cross-country
team, including the ''David from cross-country''
that Linda Jones recalled her daughter mentioning
the night of her murder. But after all the bizarre kids
they were meeting, David Graham seemed as close
to perfect as you could get at Mansfield High.

An honors student, a ROTC leader and a candidate for the Air Force Academy, Graham said he
was with his fiancée that night. And he was. He
simply left out the part about what the two of them
were doing together.

Police questioned Trisha, who seemed to be the
consensus favorite among students as Adrianne's
killer. In the attack on Adrianne's friend the year
before, Trisha had broken Kristin Clark's nose, fractured her cheekbone, given her a concussion and a
wound in the back of her head that required 45
stitches to close—all because Trisha believed Kristin had sex with her boyfriend. She had surely
proved herself capable of inflicting a deadly enough
blow to kill someone.

And there was motive, if it were true that Trisha
had threatened Adrianne after she testified against
her at a court hearing. On the way out of the courtroom, Trisha was heard to mutter to Adrianne, ''I'll
get you for this.''

It was no wonder that students kept surfacing
Trisha's name as a suspect in this case. But police

interviewed her—and her former boyfriend—and could find nothing to link her to Adrianne's murder.

While pursuing the teenagers, police also tried more traditional inductive methods of investigation. That, they felt, would be more helpful than trying to track elusive witnesses from even more intangible parties.

At the top of the ''round up the usual suspects'' list was Bill Jones himself. It was part of the routine. ''Family disturbances are still involved in a majority of homicides,'' explained Sager. ''Most victims know their assailant.''

''Our guys went in and said, 'Look, we need to have everybody cleared who possibly had an opportunity to kill your daughter,' '' recalled Chuck Sager. '' 'And that includes you. We're not here to make you mad, but we'd like you to—you don't have to do it—but we hope we have your cooperation.' ''

Bill Jones cooperated fully. And he quickly agreed to take a polygraph test. Sager was a believer in the lie detector as a win-win test. Though he knew it had limitations as a judge of the accuracy of a person's statement, he also counted on it to gauge a person's willingness to help police solve a crime. ''You run into problems when someone has something to hide,'' said Sager. ''Yeah, it may be their right not to take the test, but how many people who are innocent jump up and say, 'No, I've got a right not to do this'? When they're innocent, they go, 'How can I help you?' ''

That's what Bill Jones did. ''His kid's been killed, he knows he had an opportunity,'' recalled

Sager. "But he also knows he didn't do it, so he says, 'Yeah, I'll help you.' That's generally what you get from people when they're innocent."

Bill and Linda Jones did tell police they thought it was odd that Tracy Smith, Adrianne's current boyfriend, had not called them after the murder. As a boyfriend he was already on the "usual suspects" list, but Smith was home all that night; he too passed a polygraph.

More promising, police thought, was the lead that Smith gave them. He said that Adrianne had gotten another call while he was on the phone with her, not from a David but a Bryan. She told Tracy that it was Bryan, a boy she knew who was "depressed" and wanted to talk. A fellow worker at Golden Fried Chicken confirmed that that Sunday Adrianne had said she was meeting a Bryan later that night.

When police found a Bryan McMillen in Adrianne's address book, they were interested. Investigators were also intrigued when one of Adrianne's younger brothers said he thought he saw a pickup truck stop outside the Joneses' house late Sunday night. Bryan McMillen drove an Isuzu pickup.

Within days, police were focusing more attention on Bryan McMillen, a slight, baby-faced 17-year-old Mansfield High School dropout. His most sympathetic personality traits, however, also made him a perfect suspect; a reputation in school as a class clown, McMillen had a series of emotional and physical problems, including bronchitis and bipolar anxiety disorder.

"The McMillen kid was definitely a suspect,"

recalled one policeman close to the investigation, "because his name is Bryan, his phone number's in the book and Adrianne was going out to meet somebody named Bryan possibly."

Bryan, the youngest of three children, lived with his parents, in the same modest green brick house off South Main Street he had lived in all his life. Linda McMillen had worked as an associate principal's secretary at Mansfield High School. James McMillen was a short-haul truck driver.

Older neighbors described McMillen as quiet, churchgoing, respectful and helpful, often volunteering for chores such as moving furniture for neighbors. His major vice, according to some neighbors, was playing his electric guitar too loudly in the carport. And his only brush with the law had been over a juvenile prank. "The only time I ever know he got in trouble was for shooting off fireworks at two and three in the morning," said next-door neighbor Brian Hert, who occasionally hired McMillen for odd jobs. "It was a couple of days before the Fourth of July, and the police had come."

He had been a slightly better-than-average student at Mansfield High, and was known as a likable kid without a lot of social or extracurricular interests. His picture was not in any of his high school yearbooks, nor was he active in school sports, clubs or organizations. "He was not a discipline problem here at school at all," said principal Jerry Kirby. "He was a very quiet and reserved youngster."

Not quite *that* reserved, however. "He was the

class clown,'' said Mark Hert, 18, who knew McMillen at school and as a next-door neighbor. ''He just liked to talk. He's a nice guy, and he likes to help.''

''A couple of people said 'He's mean. How can you be friends with him?' '' a former classmate, LeAnna Fowler, 15, noted. ''But he was nice to me. He was friends with a lot of people, but he didn't click with everybody.''

Those who knew Bryan said he was just a confused kid, not a murderer. But that saw cut both ways.

He had dropped out of school in 1994, during his sophomore year, investigators learned, because he had a medical condition making him uncomfortable in crowds. Neighbors said that Bryan began having problems in school because of medication he was taking for a chemical imbalance. He told Mansfield administrators that he was going to attend a school outside the district, but they never received a request for his records.

''He didn't finish school, but he got his GED as soon as he turned 17,'' Delmer Maxwell, a next-door neighbor, said. ''There was something about large crowds. They did a lot of work with his medication, but they never did get it to where he could go to school.''

Police began to see him as a troubled boy with more problems than friends.

Even more interesting to police was that the youth worked at Eckerd's drugstore, not far from a Subway sandwich shop where Adrianne once worked. And he sometimes dropped by to see the girl. "He began to bother her so much that when she saw him coming, she started ducking her head behind the counter," recalled Linda Jones.

Twice police brought Bryan in for questioning—first, to Mansfield's police headquarters and then to Grand Prairie's. They talked to Bryan several times on the phone and visited him once at work. His father told them that Bryan was home the night of the murder.

But each time investigators talked to McMillen, they became more convinced that he was hiding something—his memory about the night of the murder was vague. They found out that he was taking four kinds of medication for clinical depression. And he told police, when they first brought him to the station for questioning, that he didn't know Adrianne Jones. When he admitted that he did know her, McMillen said he couldn't remember whether he talked to Adrianne the night of December 3. He was out drinking, he said, the first time in six months, and he had a bad reaction; got pretty drunk and couldn't remember what he did that night. Maybe he did pick Adrianne up; he couldn't recall. He was depressed because all his buddies had girlfriends, but he didn't.

When his father insisted that Bryan was at home the night of the murder and refused to let him take a lie detector test, it only encouraged police to focus more attention on Bryan. The McMillens claimed that their refusal to let him take a polygraph was the risk that their son's fragile emotional state, exacerbated by the medication he was taking, would make him a poor candidate for the test, which relied on normal reactions of people to achieve credible results. He could fail the test, even if he were innocent. Given the tone of the police questioning so far, that was a downside they didn't want to risk exposing their son to.

Investigators saw this as contrived and noncooperative. As far as they were concerned, it was looking more like *Dial M for Murder* every day: a troubled young man with a crush on a pretty and popular young woman.

What happened next would become a matter of debate—and a lawsuit. According to the McMillens, the family finally agreed to let Bryan take a lie detector test and had scheduled it for Friday, December 15, at 11:30 in the morning.

Police later denied knowledge about any such appointment. Instead, they proceeded to make plans for an arrest. On Thursday, December 14, Detective Clay called the McMillens' home and, according to James McMillen, warned him that he knew that the family wouldn't be able to afford to defend their son against what the police were "about to do." Clay added, said James McMillen, that he would make the family's life a "living hell."

That evening Clay and his colleague Dennis Meyer called local Judge Billy Mills, explaining they had a suspect in the killing of Adrianne Jones and were worried that he might be planning to flee; they needed an arrest warrant. And by 1:30 in the morning on December 15, Clay and Meyer presented Mills with an affidavit laying out their reasons for arresting McMillen.

Among other things, they claimed that McMillen had told them that Jones had been hit on the head with a hammer. "This was a fact given to us by Deputy Medical Examiner Mark Krouse of the Tarrant County Medical Examiner's Office," the officers wrote. "This was a fact which was not released to the family or press." But they also felt it important that McMillen had told them where he would have disposed of the body if he were to have committed a murder. "The description of the crime scene hypothesized by McMillen is very similar to the actual crime scene," the document said.

There was no mention in the affidavit of a scheduled polygraph test.

Mills signed the order.

Within minutes, a half-dozen police vehicles slid quietly up to the darkened house where the McMillen family had lived for 23 years. Black-uniformed figures, carrying automatic weapons equipped with laser-sighting devices, scampered across the yard. With the recent violent crime increase in Grand Prairie, the police department had established a policy of using SWAT teams on all felony arrests. And this was a capital murder warrant, the most serious felony, against a suspect that detectives considered belligerent and unpredictable; they didn't want trouble.

"This guy was possibly dangerous," recalled one of the investigators. "He was considered dangerous because of what he did to Adrianne Jones. Detectives discussed him with the FBI and the kid's personality fit the profile for committing this kind of crime. So it was a major concern that he be arrested as quickly as possible. And when you go, you don't want your police knocking on the door, people getting mad, coming out with guns and somebody getting shot.''

It was nearly 2:30 in the morning when the SWAT cops huddled quietly on the McMillens' front porch. The Christmas wreath hung pleasantly on the door. There was no noise from the inside; the family, cops hoped, was asleep.

They didn't knock—instead, with a battering ram device especially made for quick assaults, they broke open the front door and charged in. They knew the layout of the house from the investigators' previous visits and ran immediately to the bedrooms.

McMillen's parents were asleep when they heard the loud bang. But before they could even turn over, they were being pinned to their beds by men in masks, shouting at them while pushing the muzzles of weapons into their heads. Cops threw James McMillen to the floor and handcuffed his hands behind his back while other cops ripped the covers off the bed, training their weapons on a terrified Linda McMillen, who sat paralyzed in her nightgown.

Bryan too was quickly handcuffed and pulled out to the living room. He meekly protested that he had the flu and bronchitis, but police were in no mood for hearing about the health problems of the man they believed brutally murdered a teenage girl. They threw a coat over McMillen's shoulders and marched him outside, handcuffed, still barefoot, in his underwear, and shoved him into a police cruiser. With McMillen's father and mother screaming, police drove off. The teen vomited twice on the 15-mile ride to the Grand Prairie police station. His pickup truck was impounded.

"A 17-year-old drugstore clerk was arrested early Friday on charges that he fatally shot a 16-year-old Mansfield High School student earlier this month," announced the *Dallas Morning News*.

The arrest, just eleven days after the murder, was a coup for local law enforcement, which had no solid leads in the case. The suspect was in jail, held on $250,000 bail.

The Saturday headlines caused a gasp throughout the area. A gasp of relief that the killer was found; one of shock when they learned he was one of their own. James and Linda McMillen, Bryan's parents, like Adrianne's parents Linda and Bill Jones, were members of the community.

Gary Foster could now sleep. "I was scared until they arrested him," he recalled. "Several of my relatives knew Bryan McMillen's grandfather. But when they arrested him, I felt greatly relieved."

Many people knew Bryan McMillen and his family, but there was some confusion about how to react to the teenager's arrest.

"Regarding the arrest," said a stiff statement issued by Mansfield High School, "we are extremely relieved for the school community and especially

The house on Cedar Street where David Graham lived
with his mother and father.

Mansfield High School, where David Graham and Adrianne Jones met.

On the morning of December 4, 1995, the lifeless body of Adrianne Jones lay in Gary Foster's field. *(Tarrant County Medical Examiner)*

Gary Foster points to the spot where he discovered the body of Adrianne Jones.

By the time of the spring ROTC Ball, David Graham and Diane Zamora
were engaged to be married and shared a terrible secret.
(Gamma Liaison)

Memorializing Adrianne, this tree was planted by her high school friends and teachers at the edge of the school's soccer field.

Carlos and Gloria Zamora visit their Naval Cadet daughter on Parents Weekend, just a month before her arrest. *(Gamma Liaison)*

Happier times: Diane Zamora as a Girl Scout. *(Gamma Liaison)*

Most likely to succeed: David Graham when his senior picture appeared in the school yearbook. *(Don Painter Photography)*

Adrianne Jones was dead by the time her sophomore picture was published in the school yearbook. *(Don Painter Photography)*

David Graham and his Houston attorney, Dan Cogdell, during a pre-trial proceeding. *(AP/Wide World)*

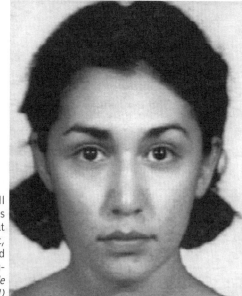

Diane Zamora, still dressed in the clothes she was sleeping in at the time of her arrest, sits for a Grand Prairie police photographer. *(AP/Wide World)*

for Adrianne's family. We felt it would be so beneficial if an arrest could be made before the holidays began.''

"Little Bryan? Little Bryan next door?" said Tina Hert, the McMillens' neighbor for six years, when told of the arrest.

"Our Bryan?" asked a cashier at Eckerd Drug in Mansfield, where Bryan worked as a clerk.

Delmer Maxwell, a next-door neighbor who had known the teenager all his life, said emphatically, "I don't think Bryan is capable of this. I don't know what the deal is, but I think they've got the wrong one," he said, adding, "I've seen the boy happy. I've seen him mad. But he didn't have a violent temper."

"They are such God-fearing people," said Donna Maxwell, Delmer Maxwell's wife. "They go to church. He went to church every Sunday with them (his parents) when he wasn't working.

"He's always been a good boy," she said. "He does what a normal 17-year-old would do. He's helpful. He's always cutting up. I cannot believe it."

Without mentioning the arrest, Linda and Bill Jones sent a letter of thanks to the local *Mansfield News-Mirror*.

"Bill and I would like to personally express our heartfelt thanks to the entire community."
"We have been living in Mansfield for 11 years and really love it here. And, now I know

why. This is one great community. The love, support and prayers sent to us were overwhelming.

"The cards, flowers, plants and many plates of food were so wonderful and beautiful. We couldn't have provided for our families and friends from out of town any better.

"The prayers sent to us from all the community churches were felt and gave us a measure of comfort during our sorrow. And, finally, the contributions to the funds were such a special help. The incredible amounts were another show of support.

"Hopefully, everyone who knew Adrianne will remember her for a long time as we will with pride and joy.

"Once again, a big Thank You for all of you from us."

The letter was signed "Bill, Linda, Justin, Scott"— and "Adrianne."

10

BETRAYAL & MURDER

"Those next weeks were horrible because I couldn't eat and neither could he," Diane Zamora would later say about the days following Adrianne Jones's murder. "He was always really jittery and pale faced. We were both afraid that each day together would be our last."

In school, David quietly endured shock over Adrianne's death. "They announced it on the intercom. My friends talked about it in the halls. Everywhere I turned, someone was crying or just staring in shock for reasons I alone was the cause of."

Yet, their years of sacrifice for lofty goals had oddly, ironically, prepared them for this suffering. They endured.

David would recall the days after the murder as "so mentally tough they make my summer at the Air Force Academy look like a walk in the park. Never have I even imagined so much guilt."

Diane too described it as hell. "I don't think anything could compare to that fear and that horrible nauseous feeling that I had all week," she recalled.

But guilt became a challenge—to be overcome.

And they called on old, familiar sources of strength. "I remember we went to church a lot," Diane later said, "praying that God would forgive us and somehow put us at peace because we were living in fear."

They had little to fear. Though questioned by police, like many other students, David Graham never fell under suspicion. He was as near perfection as it got at Mansfield High.

In fact, while Bryan McMillen was being arrested, Graham was receiving the Spaatz Award, the highest cadet honor in the Civil Air Patrol, almost guaranteeing a brilliant military career.

David and Diane gradually began to realize that they didn't have to do anything but keep quiet and stick together.

And stick they did.

"He always had both arms around her, like he was afraid she was going somewhere," recalled Diane's Aunt Sylvia. "The two of them looked like they were wrapped up in one another."

Friends and relatives noticed that the couple, instead of their ardor mellowing after the engagement announcement, grew even closer, to the exclusion of others. "He seemed more to himself," recalled Sarah Layton. "He was more quiet. But we thought it was logical. His conversations stopped. He spent more time with Zamora. He was more moody, but nobody ever thought anything about it."

Some of his friends attributed David's moodiness to his sadness over Adrianne's death. But he never talked about it.

"I love you in spite of your boyfriend," Zamora's aunt, Martha Kibler, once told Diane. "He doesn't really come across as a nice person, but if you love him, that's all I need."

Using his dad's credit card, David bought Diane and her mother leather coats for Christmas that year. He got the engagement ring out of layaway so Diane could begin wearing it, since her hand was now sufficiently healed.

"When David did come with her to some family gatherings," recalled Martha Kibler, "you couldn't even talk to Diane alone. He came over with her at either Christmas or Thanksgiving and I wanted to talk to her, to let her know how much I loved her— holiday stuff—and finally got her into the kitchen for a few seconds. Almost immediately David came in to see what we were doing."

"He didn't do it," said attorney Richard Price, a Fort Worth attorney retained by McMillen's family to represent the teen. "We can account for his time—where he was and who he was with—during the relevant time period."

Such a denial was nothing new to police. They expected it from a good defense attorney.

But Price was adamant in his denials. Though he wouldn't elaborate on McMillen's medical condition, he said the youth had "dropped out of school for a good reason, and he passed his G.E.D. with a good score." He admitted that his client had once been caught shooting off firecrackers, but that was the extent of any interaction he had with police.

"I'll say categorically that my client has not been arrested, charged or convicted in any case involving guns," said Price. "He was caught shooting firecrackers once, but that's all. Firecrackers . . . He's not a violent person. There's no tendency or any history of violence."

Price also denied the most serious allegation made by police in their arrest affidavit: that Mc-Millen mentioned a hammer blow to the head of the victim when that information had not been released to the public. In fact, Price said, his client had simply repeated what one of the police officers had told him during an earlier interrogation session.

Price also discounted the relationship between Jones and McMillen. "They weren't close friends," Price said, "and they didn't run around together or anything. He liked her and he felt terrible when she was killed. He thought it was a tragedy."

But cops were unfazed. They were confident that the forensic analysis of McMillen's truck would turn up the incriminating carpet fibers and hair strands that would link Adrianne Jones with Bryan McMillen. "Due to the materials from which Adrianne's clothes were made," boasted Detective Clay, "there should be trace evidence in the perpetrator's vehicle."

In the meantime, however, police were having a hard time convincing Bryan McMillen to confess.

At the station, they had put the teen in a padded holding cell with no bed, blanket or toilet. It measured seven feet high, seven feet long, four feet wide and had a hole in the middle of the floor for a prisoner to relieve himself. According to Mc-Millen, the room's walls and floors were littered with spit, mucous, snot, blood, pubic hair and vomit.

McMillen would later claim that he was kept in this room for the next four days, the light left on 24 hours a day; that he was fed irregularly and his "toilet" not cleaned for hours after he used it.

"If you're considered a mental health risk that's where you go," said Chuck Sager. "But he wouldn't have been in there for more than a couple of hours."

McMillen's parents brought medication for their son's bronchitis, flu and anxiety disorder to the police station, but, according to Bryan, he received it only intermittently, and rarely with enough water: only one Dixie cup's worth per day. And James and Linda McMillen recalled that they received a call during this period from someone who identified himself as one of Bryan's jailers, who told them that their son's dosage was too high and he was reducing it.

Throughout this period, while being held virtually incommunicado, McMillen said he was interrogated by various Grand Prairie police investigators, at times offering him hamburgers and french fries or a mattress to sleep on, if he would admit to the murder. They refused to let him make telephone calls. He asked for an attorney, but was told he didn't need one if he were innocent.

After four days in the Grand Prairie jail, Mc-Millen was taken to Fort Worth and incarcerated in a regular cell in the modern, six-story Tarrant County Law Enforcement Center.

And while the Grand Jury began to weigh the evidence against him, the town of Mansfield tried to make sense of McMillen's arrest.

Innocent or guilty, his incarceration compounded the town's sense of tragedy. Anna Barrett, staff writer for the *Mansfield News-Mirror,* wrote that "another teenager's family struggled with the idea their son may be involved in the crime."

Townspeople debated whether the kid they knew as sweet and gentle could have killed anyone. McMillen neighbor Lynn Marryman said, "Bryan is not capable of doing anything like that. He is a very quiet child. He doesn't bother anybody. It's hard for me to believe something like this."

"We hung out with Bryan all summer," said senior Greg Smith, 17. "Bryan was cool. He was not the type of guy to do something like that."

Even Linda Jones began to tell friends she doubted that Bryan McMillen had killed her daughter.

"I know both families," said Bryan's neighbor Lynn Marryman, "and I feel sorry for both families."

Cops were not about to relinquish their best—and only—suspect. They had been working 18-hour days on the case and had already interviewed dozens of people. There was no one else. But they were also striking out in their search for evidence against McMillen.

They brought in crime-scene experts to go over

McMillen's truck, looking for any sign—hair, clothing fibers, dirt, guns, bullets—that proved Adrianne Jones's presence in that truck. They found nothing. Nor did anything analyzed by Forensic Consultant Services from McMillen's home connect him with the crime.

And police still could find no murder weapon or blunt object—or motive beyond that which was locked in Bryan McMillen's head.

As the tests progressed, McMillen spent Christmas and New Year's in jail; his attorney, meanwhile, worked out another agreement for him to take a lie detector test. He passed.

Finally, the Tarrant prosecutor's office concluded they could no longer hold McMillen. "We had some forensic examinations done, and there was no indication they connected him to the offense," announced Alan Levy, chief of the criminal division for the district attorney's office. On the polygraph, said Levy, McMillen "was asked three specific questions" and passed—"and he didn't pass by a little bit, he passed by a lot." Said Levy, "I'm satisfied there isn't evidence that he had anything to do with it."

The murder charge was dropped. And McMillen was released on January 7, after three weeks in jail.

The *Fort Worth Star Telegram* called the release "a major setback for Grand Prairie police." That was an understatement; police had exhausted their suspects and their leads.

"Are we frustrated?" Sergeant Doug Clancey said. "Sure we are."

Investigators defended themselves, some even suggesting, anonymously, that they thought prosecutors had made a mistake in releasing McMillen. Some residents were not convinced that McMillen didn't commit the murder. "Even after they released him," recalled Gary Foster, "I thought he did it. I felt that they would have had to have had enough information to arrest."

Despite the lack of hard evidence, police believed McMillen's statement about "the hammer" was crucial. "That was a key piece of information," said Clancey. "No investigator told him that. If we let out all the information we had, it makes our case much harder to solve."

"It's frustrating and it's unfortunate," said Clancey. "We were convinced he was the one. We're regrouping, but at this point we can't rule anything out"—including, admitted some cops, Bryan McMillen.

"There were 50 to 60 pieces of evidence from the truck," Clancey said. "Not all of those were looked at by the D.A. They [detectives] feel they need to still look at that."

Assistant D.A. Levy wasn't especially happy to learn that Grand Prairie police were clinging to McMillen. "My understanding is the police don't consider him an active suspect," he said.

"They still think they've got the right guy," a source told the *Fort Worth Star Telegram.*

Those suggestions only made McMillen and his family more angry than they already were. "The evidence never pointed to Bryan," said attorney

Richard Price. "It was incredibly bad police work that led to his arrest." And Price gave notice that Grand Prairie police might indeed get a chance to see Bryan McMillen in court—but as defendants in a wrongful arrest suit.

"They just took the easy way out," said Price. "It was a high-profile case. My client's name was mentioned. Someone said Adrianne said she received a call from Bryan. But there are a lot of Bryans in Mansfield. Other than that, there was no evidence to indicate he was 'the' Bryan. . . . The district attorney's office did a good job. It's just a shame that the Grand Prairie police department jumped at the first suspect they saw and put all their emphasis on trying to get a confession from him."

The day after Bryan McMillen's release Grand Prairie City Manager Gary Gwyn announced an order to review the police tactical squad. "I know there are times when the use of force is totally justified, especially when you have narcotics involved," said Gwyn. "But I have had some questions about what the threshold and degree of evidence is for using this type of force."

Police felt victimized by politics. "The city fathers hate bad publicity," said one cop. "Don't matter what the police department does, you just better not read about it in the newspaper."

The mayor, Charles England, admitted as much. Recalling the controversy surrounding the arrest of an African-American bank executive who was handcuffed after being pulled over for a routine traffic violation, he said, "I'm concerned any time there is negative publicity about this city, whether it's the police department or any other department. We've had conversations with the city manager and the manager with the police chief to find out if they are isolated incidents or if they are a problem."

Opined the *Fort Worth Star Telegram:*

Grand Prairie's leadership took a wise step Tuesday in deciding to review the way the police department's tactical team is used in making arrests.

The inspiration for City Manager Gary Gwyn's action was the brutish arrest of 17-year-old Bryan McMillen last month in the murder of 16-year-old Mansfield honor student Adrianne Jones.

Tactical squad officers from Grand Prairie smashed in the front door of McMillen's parents' home at 2:30 A.M. Dec. 15 and carried him off to jail. Last week McMillen passed a polygraph examination, and the charge of murder filed against him was dropped for lack of evidence.

Gwyn and Mayor Charles England are right to be worried about aspects of their police department. If Grand Prairie police were so estranged from reality as to imagine an urgent need to batter down a quiet family's front door

*in the middle of the night, then it is hardly
surprising that their grounds for arresting and
charging McMillen were so insubstantial.*

Grand Prairie police, embarrassed both by
McMillen's release and the criticism of their investigation, were on the defensive. "Everything was on
the up and up," said Sergeant Clancey. "I really
can't comment beyond that. We provided our reasons for the arrest procedure and that was reviewed."

"I feel bad for [McMillen] to have to go through
that—for his family," Cathy Britton said. "I hope
they find who did it. I hope they don't just sweep
it under the carpet."

In fact, there was very little anymore to sweep
under the carpet. Bryan McMillen had been their
best—and only—suspect. "I wouldn't say we're
going to go back to square one," Sergeant Clancey
said. "We're going to go back to actively investigating and reviewing our notes to make sure we
didn't miss anything."

"We'll probably be guarded," Clancey said
about the future of the investigation. "We'll make
sure every I is dotted and every T is crossed. . . . I
think [the Jones family] would like to put this to
rest."

"I knew they had the wrong guy all along,"
Linda Jones said. "So I kept being the way that I
was—not judgmental, not raising Cain. Right now,
I'm just dealing with it."

Cops seemed to have forgotten about Linda

Jones's saying her daughter got a call from David from cross-country. They seemed not to have suspected that Adrianne may not have wanted to tell Tracy Smith about someone she may have liked.

Instead, the rumor mill picked up again. The killer was again "at large," whether it was Bryan McMillen or Trisha or someone else. "We were constantly hearing that girl's name as a suspect," recalled Chuck Sager. "And she finally got an attorney, and the attorney said, let's take the polygraph. Even her boyfriend, who was an adult out of Fort Worth, was polygraphed."

"She aced it," said her attorney, David Chapman. "She had no involvement and no knowledge of who is involved. . . . She had been convicted in the court of public opinion by the gossipmongers in Mansfield. She said if she passed, she wanted people to know she passed."

"Weeks of rumor and gossip . . . ended," said the *Mansfield News-Mirror*.

But the paper also editorialized on the front page, "a killer remains at large in the community." Worse, it said, leads were drying up; "fewer tips are being noted through the Crimestoppers hotline."

"What remains," said the paper, "is a murder trail that grows colder with each hour. Detectives Dennis Clay and Dennis Meyer continue reviewing key elements of the case. 'There's nothing new,' he said again. 'We wish we could say more. There's nothing new.' "

The paper repeated the circumstances of Adrianne Jones's death, hopeful that the information

would jog a memory, scare out a clue or a guilty
conscience confession: "The Mansfield High
School honor student and cross-country athlete had
been shot twice in the face and head and struck once
on the head with a blunt object. The girl was found
wearing dark blue-and-green plaid flannel shorts, a
gray t-shirt with the 'UIL Region-I Cross-Country
Regionals 1995' logo and a V-neck Nike pullover,
police said. Jones had no shoes on when her body
was found."

The cross-country regionals was an event that
David Graham remembered well. He was at that
meet, in Lubbock. But he was not considered a suspect.

In fact, the perfect union between two talented
youngsters was increasingly an isolating one. David
and Diane stopped double-dating and going to family and friends' parties as often; and when they did
go, they stayed to themselves. They seemed even
less concerned about missing Tuesday evening
C.A.P. meetings.

David went to Diane's house every afternoon after school to run with her. He often stayed so late
that he fell asleep on the couch. His father would
call, angry, but David seemed in no rush to get
home.

"Diane wanted to go back," David later said of
Diane's mood after the murder. "For weeks her infatuation was with just being able to go back before
September 26 when she wrecked my truck and injured her hand. She wanted to change that and she

wanted to keep me from going to Lubbock. Diane was constantly depressed from the guilt. She was also scared that I would be arrested. She used to worry herself sick in school over me and have to call me as soon as school was out to make sure I was OK.''

He wasn't okay. He watched Adrianne's friends grieve. He saw Adrianne's family in town. But he read the stories in the newspaper about the investigation, which was going nowhere fast.

11

DEAD ENDS

At the end of January 1996, Grand Prairie Police Chief Harry Crum reported to his city council, "We're not any closer to making an arrest."

"It is an active investigation," said police spokesman Clancey, "but there are very few, if any, leads."

It was the same in February. March. April. May.

Linda Jones was frustrated—and said so.

"I feel like basically they're at a dead-end and they don't know where to go from here," she told the *Fort Worth Star Telegram*. Every murder case seemed to be solved but her daughter's. "They found the murderers of Jeff Doolittle [a man killed in March], they found the murderers and the culprits of so many other cases, like the taxi cab driver. Why isn't mine being solved? What is it so weird? Why is it so bizarre? Andy Kline's [killed in February] was solved two days later. Why not mine?"

Jones wondered aloud about whether Grand Prairie police should even be involved in the case. "If it would have been two more blocks this way, it would have been handled by Mansfield," she said.

"That's all it would have taken—two blocks—to have it handled by Mansfield police who know us and would have investigated harder. . . . I want the people in Mansfield handling it. They already have all the 'ins' and 'outs' on most of the people in Mansfield."

By now Grand Prairie police were wishing they could give it to Mansfield. Dennis Clay and Dennis Meyer had moved back to their own offices as soon as McMillen was arrested on December 15. And they had no inclination—no reason—to move back after his release. Detectives went back to working other cases and they met with Mansfield police once a week to talk about progress—mostly, about the lack of it.

The pace of the investigation was all the more disheartening for Linda Jones because she believed that the answers were in Mansfield. "Adrianne is a Mansfield person with Mansfield connections," she told the *Star Telegram.* "A friend has murdered her and is out there roaming the streets. I hope guilt eats them up."

It was. David Graham saw that story and it "haunted me," he later recalled. "When I read that, I just wanted it to all go away. I wanted to able to drive Adrianne back home, to go to sleep and to wake up back on December 3 free to make decisions all over again."

Alone, David and Diane fought; they yelled, they screamed, they kicked. They didn't want to be together, but they couldn't escape each other.

Sometimes they seemed to flinch from the stabbing pain of guilt, their secret close to bubbling to the surface.

"I remember her telling me how David would get mad at her for things," recalled Mary Mendoza. "Then she added, 'But that's all right.' I asked her why she was going to get married and her response to me was that she wasn't a liar. I didn't understand what she was saying until she explained, saying, 'I told him I was going to marry him and I'm going to keep my word.' "

What Diane didn't tell her aunt was how much more than yelling was involved.

"Diane told us that she and her boyfriend beat each other up," recalled an Annapolis friend of Zamora's.

What they hid under the veil of love and success was their dark deed—and they tortured each other with it, as if it were a cleansing ritual to help them cope with the outside world.

"She showed us a scar on her knee, telling us that it was from one of their knife fights," said the Annapolis friend. "On one occasion, she said David put a belt around her neck and tried to choke her. He had claw marks on his neck from when she tried to choke him to death."

When the Zamoras went to a mall restaurant on Easter Sunday, four months after the murder, Diane brought David. "It was impossible to even hold a conversation with her when he wasn't around," recalled Mary Mendoza. "He was always watching her, always very protective."

Occasionally, the anger and violence showed itself, however meekly, to outsiders.

"She was very standoffish, and snooty, and she made David cold and standoffish," Sarah Layton recalled. "If you got David away from her and her away from David, they were totally different people. But if you got them together, David was more quiet and she was more edgy and tense." The last thing anyone suspected was an edginess caused by murder. Like most of their friends, Layton guessed that, "she was wanting to control him or was just insecure. . . . She was just rude to people, totally rude to people that she didn't even know and there was no reason to be rude to."

David, too, got testier with friends, warning them not to mention other girls in Diane's presence. Never very pushy about his accomplishments, he seemed even more remote his senior year. In the school yearbook, despite his scholastic and military honors, he was not even mentioned in the senior achievements section. On a page celebrating the school's ROTC program, Graham, though he was the highest-ranking student and Battalion Commander, was not pictured.

Diane was no longer as bubbly and outgoing as she was before meeting David. And while David seemed aggressive and arrogant, Diane seemed unconcerned about his behavior. It alarmed the family that she once allowed David to lay on top of her, seductively, in front of her grandparents at their house.

All of this change was attributed, in the eyes of

friends and relatives, to their "love." It didn't make sense, it didn't even seem healthy. But it was, everyone kept reminding each other, love.

"After he came along," complained Diane's aunt, Martha Kibler, "there was no getting her by herself. And he was always very disrespectful to my mom and dad. He wouldn't even say hello to them."

The only member of the Zamora family that David seemed to get along with was a brother-in-law, Ross Fowler, who liked guns. "When David found out about that, they talked guns quite a bit," recalled Sylvia Gonzalez.

"We knew they planned to be together and get married," Sarah Layton recalled, "so we just hoped she would get over it and they could be happy. And that's all we wanted. We weren't going to say anything to upset him."

Amy Franklin recalled the time Diane reproached her at a picnic for letting David help her to her feet during a Junior ROTC exercise. "She said, 'He's not supposed to touch females. He's not supposed to touch anybody,'" Franklin recalled. "She started yelling at him. She jumped all over him."

David and Diane both applied for a job at Wal-Mart in Mansfield; but when only David was hired, Diane persuaded him to quit. "She controlled most of his life," said Sarah Layton. "She even got him to quit a couple of jobs because she said it took time away from her."

"He was on a short leash," recalled Amy Franklin, another Junior ROTC member.

But Diane's friends and relatives thought that it was David who pulled the leash. "He smothered her," said Gonzalez. "He'd say, 'She's got to do what I tell her to do.' "

"She seemed to change all of a sudden after she met him," recalled Mary Mendoza.

If they could just make it to graduation, maybe there would be some respite.

Linda Jones too was trying to make it. "There's a sense of acceptance now, not the total disbelief like at first," Jones said in April. "We're returning to a normalcy, but it's a changed normalcy."

She allowed *Mansfield News-Mirror* reporter Anna Barrett and *Fort Worth Star Telegram* writer Deanna Boyd to come to the house for interviews and, though never having been a community activist, she also made many rounds of public meetings— a vivid and troublesome reminder of the fact that her daughter's killer was still at large.

"I'm still in shock that such a violent crime could happen here in Mansfield," she told people at a breakfast meeting of the Mansfield Chamber of Commerce. She proposed that the town start a mentoring program for local teens. "My hope is, you start questioning your own youth," she said. "When this all happened and the police started questioning us, we began to see that we knew so little about our daughter's friends or the people who she went to parties with."

Once just a massage therapist and mother, Linda Jones was now a symbol and an activist. "We can defeat this criminal element," she said. "We have got to do it."

She found a theme, expressed first around the tree planted with Adrianne's friends behind the soccer field. "Unity, strength and courage. These are the three words I want to leave with you today," she would say. "Unity so that we can come together. Strength is for the power that unity creates. And courage to take on the problems of the present."

People listened. They were glad that she was keeping her daughter's memory alive.

"One thing that was good was that Adrianne's mother was real active in keeping it public," recalled Gary Foster. "She was real active the entire time. There was a portable sign up in town asking for information. There were ads in the local paper offering a reward. She would write letters to the editor. She did a lot of things to keep people thinking about it."

A picture of Adrianne's two brothers playing with the family's German shepherd dog ran on the front page of the Mansfield paper.

"We try to do a lot together," said Linda. "I really don't know what to tell you about what we're going through."

Adrianne's death fell especially hard on her two younger brothers. "Adrianne was there on the bed when he was delivered," Linda said of the youngest, Scott, now 11. "There's always been an extremely close tie between them." Scott, a fifth grader at Mary Orr Intermediate, "is learning to cope with anger that bubbles to the surface on occasion," wrote Anna Barrett.

Barrett described Justin, 13, a seventh grader at Rogene Worley Middle School, as a "perpetual motion machine, eager to keep active, desperate to occupy time." Both boys said they were managing and that most of their friends were "cool" about Adrianne's death. "It does bother me when I hear someone say something like 'I hate my sister. I wish she was dead,' " Justin told Barrett. "They have no idea when their sister's gonna be dead."

"They don't come outside as much, they don't walk the dog as much, they don't converse with people like they used to," next-door neighbor Jessica Ramon recalled.

Gradually, the family packed up some of Adrianne's belongings; they gave most of them to family and friends or the Mansfield Women's Shelter. Bill Jones got rid of the old truck he and Adrianne were restoring. "I couldn't look at it anymore," he said.

"People have so many things. You don't know what was special to them that you should keep," said Linda. "I have got things that we're always going to keep; her favorite dress, her scarf that she always ran in, her running shoes, her soccer cleats, her stereo, some of her makeup.

"You just can't sell the things that were special to them or that they kept. There's no value that can be placed on it at this point."

Every day Linda wore something that belonged to Adrianne; mascara or shoes or shirts. She made numerous pilgrimages to the murder site, spreading dried flower petals over the ground, secretly hoping to meet her daughter's killer there.

Gradually, she also noted that there were now moments when she wasn't thinking about her daughter. "I was so proud of myself the other day," she said, nearly six months after Adrianne's death. "I had a new client come in, and I didn't even talk about it at all."

And though they could take things out of Adrianne's room, they couldn't put anything new in it. "The room isn't a shrine," said Linda. "I just haven't had the gumption to go in there and change it into something else yet.

"Adrianne is, and always will be, part of our family," said Linda. "She is simply in another form now."

Bill Jones remained a sideline figure throughout, "deeply hurt," said Barrett. Though he wanted to grab every teenager in town and question them, he instead threw himself into his work. "That's his therapy," said Linda. "We don't talk about her a whole lot. Bill doesn't ever want to."

Many people, including the police, continued to believe that Bryan McMillen would slip up and confess. But it was a theory of guilt spawned as much by the absence of evidence as by its presence. There was no one else.

"We all just kind of felt like it was not ever going to be resolved," recalled Merilyn Gerloff, a senior vice president at the Overton Bank, which had offered the reward for information about Adrianne's murder. "I never dreamed that they would ever, ever find the girl's murderer."

"Eventually, I just thought it was a dead case and they wouldn't catch anyone," said Gary Foster.

Adrianne's death continued to haunt her friends, who spent hours talking about the murder, testing each other's theories about who had killed their friend, "obsess[ing] about the details of the crime as if they were unraveling a plot from *The X-Files*," as Ellise Pierce wrote in the *Dallas Observer*.

Tina Dollar, manager of Golden Fried Chicken, had to replace her entire staff after Adrianne died. "She was my star," recalled Dollar. "Nobody was smiling at the customers anymore. I had to hire a new crew just to get the morale back up."

"The days will have healed all the cries and the moans, but we will never forget sweet Adrianne Jones," went the small poem written by Robert Hubbard in the Mansfield High yearbook for that year.

One of Adrianne's friends painted a portrait of Adrianne in art class. She recalled showing it to David Graham, who sat behind her in a government class. "You did a good job, April," was his only comment.

Sometimes just coping with the sudden and violent loss of a friend was difficult. Kristin Clark had nightmares for months after Adrianne's death. It was too close to her own brush with death. She temporarily escaped into cocaine that spring and wished she could escape Mansfield too.

Police seemed equally resigned to getting on with life. "We want closure just like the families," said Doug Clancey. But with no new leads, they were grabbing at straws more than following leads. "Somebody knows what happened," said Clancey. "There could be any new evidence that could come forward. Maybe an eyewitness can answer the questions."

Perhaps. But by June of 1996, investigators with the Grand Prairie police decided to put the case on a back burner. They had interviewed nearly 300 people and, except for the arrest of Bryan McMillen, had gotten nowhere. Detective Dennis Clay was still assigned to follow up on any leads—but none came in. The local paper kept running small stories about the case; each time giving the phone number to call with information. But no one called.

And there were only so many stories the local papers could do about nothing; other news kept crowding Adrianne's murder out of the headlines. Good news—about the three Mansfield students who earned awards from the Poetry Society of Texas, about the 42 students from Mansfield High who earned the University Interscholastic League Scholar Award. And some bad news—about a $3.6 million loss of state funding for the schools. And dull news—the "Loop 9" project that would bring a major interstate highway to the northern edge of town was on track. But never news about Adrianne Jones's killer.

Worried that the dearth of press coverage signaled an end to the chance for leads, Bill and Linda

Jones used their own money to buy and post signs in town.

City Manager Clayton Chandler waived the fees on the sign the Joneses put up in the parking lot of the Winn-Dixie, on the road leading to the high school.

$REWARD$ 469-TIPS
INFO FOR ARREST OF
PERSON INVOLVED IN
ADRIANNE JONES CASE

June was an especially hard month for the Jones family. Instead of preparing for their daughter's 17th birthday, they thought only about her death. "This is a particularly hard time for us," said Linda Jones. "Adrianne's birthday is June 18, so we're having a little trouble with that." There would be no dances or proms or graduations. There would be no looking forward to college or career or parenthood.

June was the month Adrianne's schoolmates were moving on—to better things, to other things, to something. Anything. Youth had its promise, its hope, its expectation. Death had nothing.

12

ACADEMY BOUND

While keeping her daughter's memory alive was difficult for Linda Jones, it was the good news stories about other kids that were most bittersweet. They were reminders of her loss.

Stories like the one about three Mansfield students winning a University Interscholastic League Scholar Award, a prize Linda Jones knew her daughter was in the running for; just as she knew that Adrianne was wearing her UIL t-shirt when she was murdered.

David Graham was one of the most feted Mansfield students in 1996. He was a UIL scholar, an honors student and, finally, recipient of a prestigious appointment to the United States Air Force Academy.

No one was surprised by Graham's accomplishments. A citizens panel had reviewed all the applications to the service academies from Congressman Martin Frost's district—evaluating SAT scores, class rank and recommendations from counselors, teachers and advisors—and recommended David for an appointment.

Graham got word of his appointment the same day that Diane Zamora received news that she was accepted into the U.S. Naval Academy. "We went out to celebrate his appointment and we didn't even check the mail to see if I got mine," Diane recalled. "When we got home, we called his mom to tell her I got nominated too. She couldn't believe it. It was a real surprise."

Diane's acceptance seemed no less predestined. And though she would tell people she knew "what an honor it is to get this appointment to the Naval Academy," she also appreciated the fact that it was free. "It's been hard on my parents financially," she told Nancy Huckaby, a reporter for the *Crowley Review*. If it weren't for the Academy appointment—which came with free room and board in return for a promise on her part to spend at least four years in the Navy—she couldn't afford to go to any college.

Nancy Huckaby was one of the first to see the potential of a story about Diane Zamora. An editor for the local *Crowley Review*, she first saw Zamora's name on a list of students being honored at Awards Day at the high school that spring. "It was odd that I had never heard of Diane Zamora," Huckaby recalled. "Usually, by then, someone has called me before to let me know that their son or daughter is getting an award. The congressional office will call. Even the kids themselves will call."

Huckaby had lived in Crowley for more than a decade and had a daughter almost Zamora's age. "It was kind of odd that I'd never heard of her before.

Usually, you hear about the real smart kids by the time they leave high school. They've done something else to merit attention—gotten awards at scientific fairs, won national merit scholarships, honors societies, some other awards. And you can track these kids through grade school, middle school, right through high school. So, when I heard of this girl going to the Naval Academy, I just thought it was funny that I'd never heard of her. But when I saw her name, I knew that was a story for us and called the school."

The school was happy to give Huckaby Diane's phone number. And the reporter called to set up an interview. This was that rare story that everyone—parents, school officials *and* newspapers—loved. So Huckaby was somewhat surprised when the teenager told her she'd rather not do the interview at her house.

"Most of the time, you call them up and they say come by the house," recalled Huckaby. "The parents want to be involved in these kinds of stories. But Diane wanted to meet at the high school."

Huckaby didn't press the issue and went ahead and arranged to talk to Diane in a conference room at the high school. "She was petite and attractive," Huckaby recalled thinking when the young prospective Annapolis cadet entered the room. "But she wasn't wearing any makeup and didn't have her hair done. I had told her I was bringing a photographer, but now she said she didn't want her picture taken."

Huckaby proceeded with her interview and the

story ran under a front-page banner headline, "CHS [Crowley High School] Grad Earns Appointment to U.S. Naval Academy at Annapolis." "Senior overcomes injuries from auto accident to pass stringent physical fitness requirements," read the second headline. And it ran with a "glam" picture that Diane had dropped off, a studio portrait that looked nothing like a military cadet in the making. In the picture, signed "Marcel's," Zamora leans forward, resting her chin on her crossed arms, looking pensively into the camera. Her pouty lips were painted, her arms and shoulders bare. She wore dangly earrings, with her long black hair fixed on her head, except for a tantalizing curl that looped dangerously—sensually—close to her right eye.

It seemed to Huckaby that Zamora spent most of the interview praising David Graham. She seemed genuinely humbled by the honor of going to the Naval Academy, but Huckaby thought, as she later said, "it was kind of odd that her family didn't have any military history. Usually, there was some family history common among those who go to the academies."

But every attempt to find out about Zamora's family was met with evasion. "I couldn't get much out of her about her family," recalled Huckaby. "I asked about the major influences in her life and everything was David. She gave the impression that she couldn't have done anything without David Graham."

The only other credits went to God. "I have never been a religious person," she told Huckaby, oddly forgetting her years at her grandfather's Templo, "but I really owe so much to God. He helped me so much through all that. There is no way I could have pulled through that without Him."

Zamora said she couldn't be a pilot because she was too short and her eyesight was not quite perfect. "While her eyes may not be 'perfect,' " Huckaby concluded, "they were able to see a perfect opportunity when it came her way—an opportunity this young Crowley senior is not about to let pass her by."

That spring David threw himself into the planning for the ROTC ball in May, a gala affair at the Woodlawn Country Club in Fort Worth. He worried about every detail, which was very Davidlike. But Diane came to the ball and David became a different person.

One of David's friends recalled talking with Diane and Adrianne Jones's name came up. "I despise her with a passion," said Diane and stormed off.

Each high school had a special ceremony to honor Diane and David's achievements. "They made a really big deal," said Shane Johnson about Zamora's Naval Academy honors.

Diane went to Mansfield High to be with David when he was presented with his Air Force Academy acceptance letter and was at his side as the student body gave him a long ovation. "I know this sounds strange to say now," recalled Becki Strosnider, the editor of the school's newspaper, the *Mansfield Uproar*, "but we thought it was so cool that he had followed his dream."

David came to Diane's graduation. It was an end of May event, a Wednesday evening, at Daniel-Meyer Coliseum on the campus of Texas Christian University in Fort Worth. Salutatorian Josie Stewart told her 300 graduating classmates and their hundreds of relatives that "Friends play an essential and unique role in our lives. Friends divide your sorrows and multiply your joys." And valedictorian Brandi Jutson told the crowd, "We must all find our place in the world. We are all capable of great things."

Principal Bill Johnson, studying the list of outstanding students in the class, asked someone to point out the girl who got the appointment to the Naval Academy. It was odd, since he would normally know someone who seemed as accomplished as she was, but he couldn't picture Diane Zamora in his mind.

Speeches were delivered. The Mighty Eagle Band played. And diplomas were presented. First, to Alvin Lee Adair; last to Diane Michelle Zamora.

But for some of Diane's family, the ceremony was marred by David Graham. "He never took his arm from around her," recalled her Aunt Martha. "Several members of the family wanted to give her a hug, but David wouldn't let go of her. I finally said, 'Hey, she's my niece and I'm going to give her a hug.' He just sort of looked at me, didn't say anything, but stepped aside for a few seconds."

Diane's mother, however, knew how good the real story was. Of 8,736 who applied to the Air Force Academy from all over the United States, only 1,239 were admitted. Of nearly 10,000 who had wanted to go to Annapolis, only 1,212 were accepted.

She called the *Fort Worth Star Telegram* to tell them. It was a good story. And the paper dispatched Rosanna Ruiz, a reporter from the paper's Spanish-language section called "La Estrella," to interview the couple.

Ruiz spent hours with Zamora and Graham at Graham's house in Mansfield. Her timing was perfect, catching the couple just before they were departing for their new Academy lives.

He already had "the look of a military man with his razor-short haircut," the reporter observed, "and two days before he was set to leave, his anticipation was more than obvious."

Diane was "help[ing] him pack up," though dressed in a dark mini-skirt, sweater and stockings, she was also ready for the press.

Ruiz found out that David had received a nomination to West Point from Vice President Al Gore and noted his comment, "I didn't want to be in the Army," with an observation that he said it "with a squinched-up nose."

There was Graham, perusing an Air Force Academy brochure, smiling as he asked, "Isn't that a beautiful campus?"

Graham was one of only 1,000 students accepted to the Academy and was considered one of their best candidates. "He is in the top five percent of all Class of 2000 cadets," Lieutenant Colonel Doug McCoy said. "They look at the whole cadet when they make that ranking—academics, athletics and community activities when they were high school students: if they're involved in ROTC or Key Club or student council.''

And the video tapes and books that he and Diane were putting into a box were going to storage—not to Colorado Springs. "You're only supposed to take the clothes on your back," he told Ruiz.

Diane told the reporter that she had initially wanted to go to the Air Force Academy as well, but changed her mind about applying after suffering injuries to her fingers in a serious accident in September. The Navy's deadlines were later so she applied to Annapolis. Zamora said she has taken advanced courses in high school to prepare herself, but she knows the Academy will be tough.

Ruiz wondered how the couple thought they could keep a long-distance relationship together for the next four years. "They are quick to note that they have holidays and spring breaks to share," Ruiz reported.

"There's always e-mail, it's free," Diane told the reporter. "So we won't have huge long-distance bills."

But Ruiz couldn't help but press the two about how they thought they could keep their relationship going until the year 2000. "I was surprised at how adamant they were," she recalled. "They said they were certain the marriage was going to happen and that there were not going to be any outs. Then they stopped and looked at one another."

"If she hangs in with him for four years, maybe it was meant to be," said Gloria Zamora, Diane's mother, seeming remarkably resigned for such a public utterance. "I remember being her age and that's when I got married."

"I said to her, 'What if you get killed doing that?' " Gloria told Ruiz. "And she told me, 'I'll get killed doing what I love to do.' . . . I always knew that she would do what she said she would."

Ten days after Adrianne Jones's birthday, the *Fort Worth Star Telegram* story was published: "Couple to march to military drums, then wedding bells."

It was the kind of story that made people feel good. It was love. It was youth. It was discipline and achievement and redemption; the redemption small towns feel—celebrate, honor, applaud—whenever one of their sons or daughters succeeds beyond the town's borders.

The accompanying picture showed a fresh-scrubbed teenage boy and girl, in a living room, putting items in a box. Packing. Getting ready to leave. The room, some in Mansfield knew, was that of Jerry and Janice Graham. The "Jesus" plaque hung prominently above the family pictures, on a white-paneled wall.

David left for Colorado Springs on June 30. Diane would go to Annapolis on July 2, then, as Ruiz wrote, "on to the rest of her life."

13

THE LAST CONFESSION

David and Diane left their hometowns that summer with the righteous fanfare of explorers. And word soon came back that they had arrived and were surviving their summer boot camps—the final rigorous entry exam, designed to weed out some of the weaker "plebes" (Navy) and "doolies" (Air Force) before the really rough stuff began in the fall.

On August 1, a Friday, after less than five weeks of intense physical tests, David, along with 1170 other freshmen (966 men and 204 women), was made an official Air Force cadet, fourth class. As a member of the Class of 2000, he was in the home stretch of his lifelong race to become an Air Force pilot—now only four years away.

He joined the cadet honor guard, something totally familiar to him from his Junior ROTC days, and began receiving his cadet pay of $558.04 per month. This was in addition to the fully paid tuition and room and board that Graham was to receive for the next four years. But, as the Air Force was quick to point out, after deducting for the miscellaneous expenses of haircuts, laundry, school books, etc., that didn't leave much for pocket money. Better still, if Graham left the Academy before his junior year, he was under no obligation to return the money; it was truly "pay." Beginning with the junior year, however, it was up to the Secretary of the Air Force to decide what would have to be paid back.

Meanwhile, Diane wrote home to say she was going to join the Navy choir.

David seemed to do fine. But Diane, despite hopeful letters, was suffering. Physically and emotionally.

There was nothing about the stately campus on the banks of the Chesapeake Bay that hinted at the pressure it would put on students, four thousand of them wanting to be Naval officers.

Diane was one of 9,962 who applied for admission to the Naval Academy class of 2000 and one of only 200 female freshman who marched onto the 338-acre campus, or Yard, on the banks of the Severn River. On these grounds John Paul Jones was buried. Since 1845, when Secretary of State George Bancroft first opened the school's doors, the Academy had produced a President of the United States (Jimmy Carter), not to mention thousands of Naval and Marine officers who had gone to war, many of them not returning.

Ten percent of those who walked onto the Yard with Diane that hot July would not survive the six weeks of hell known as "plebe summer."

Tourists flocked to the Academy on weekends to

gaze at the imposing granite building, the velvety lawns and the midshipmen in their crisp white uniforms. And there was much to be awed by at this 151-year-old institution.

But Zamora was also entering a troubled institution. Cheating scandals and sex scandals had taken some of the luster off the marbled columns. And in one two-week period just the previous April a midshipman and four former students were arrested as part of a car-theft ring; another student was jailed for sexually assaulting four women students; another was charged with (and later pleaded guilty to) fondling a toddler, the granddaughter of a couple who were part of an Academy hospitality program; and two midshipmen were arrested after crawling through the window of one of the men's former girlfriend (whose father happened to be the former state police superintendent); another student was court-martialed for LSD use.

Diane was only remotely aware of the scandals as she moved into Bancroft Hall, an imposing white building at the center of the campus and one of its largest dormitories, co-ed, with 1,875 rooms. If she survived the next six weeks, she would be sworn in, a Naval officer, at Tecumseh Court in front of Bancroft. In a few weeks, when the upperclass men and women arrived, the court would be dotted with 4,000 uniformed young men and women at each midday formation, complete with color guard and a band playing the Navy and Marine Corps anthems as everyone marched to lunch.

For now, it was just the freshmen, starting plebe

summer, the torturous boot camp that served as an initiation to the Navy. Over the next six weeks, Diane would be subjected to 100 hours of exercise, marching, shooting, sailing and saying, "ma'am" and "sir" at the end of each and every sentence, during a day that began at 5:30 in the morning and ended at ten in the evening.

She learned to square corners on her bed, memorize hundreds of pages of Naval Academy facts and the first names and hometowns of every member of her platoon, to be recited whenever an officer requested it.

Within days she would know the Naval Academy honor code by heart:

Midshipmen are persons of integrity: they stand for that which is right. They tell the truth and ensure that the full truth is known. They do not lie. They embrace fairness in all action. They ensure that work submitted as their own is their own, and that assistance received from any source is authorized and properly documented. They do not cheat. They respect the property of others and ensure that others are able to benefit from the use of their own property. They do not steal.

More than 80 plebes dropped out after just four weeks. Diane was hurting, but wanted to stay.

"She liked to talk about David," recalled Jay Guild, a plebe from Illinois, who became her squad leader. "She missed him a lot. She often talked about him very strangely, as if she didn't trust him, but she still wanted to be with him. It was very odd." Diane had "crying fits," according to Guild, when David didn't answer her e-mail.

Like Zamora, Guild was a high school standout reared in a fractured family. His father, Roland, lived in Oklahoma and Jay lived with his mother in Kankakee, Illinois, where he was an honor roll student and member of the National Honor Society, the engineering club and the varsity wrestling team. He was also an Illinois State Scholar, making him one of the top ten percent of graduating seniors in the state; as well as a recipient of the Presidential Award for Academic Excellence, an honor that came with being among the top two percent of the country's high schoolers.

The kudos for Guild sounded much like those heaped upon Graham and Zamora. "He was an excellent student," recalled Kankakee high school principal, Linda Yonke. "He was very personable, very nice. He was one of our top students."

And like Graham and Zamora, Guild's dreams focused on the military. He knew that after Annapolis, he wanted to be a Marine. On his mother's answering machine in Kankakee, his voice could be heard belting out the Marine Corps anthem. "My Ma-rine Corps, colors of green, just to show them we are mean," ending with a solemn "*Semper Fi*," the Marines' motto, "Always Faithful."

And in Guild, Zamora found a faithful friend. She needed one desperately as the rigors of plebe summer exacted their price.

For the mandatory plebe autobiographical sketch, she turned in an essay that didn't mention any of her accomplishments and ambitions. Instead, she wrote only about David Graham and her engagement. "That was just bizarre," said one Academy official.

She also stood out by not participating in the community outreach program that all the plebes were expected to join. Under the program, families in the Annapolis area served as "sponsors" of midshipmen to help them adjust to the rigors of Academy life. Twice Zamora was assigned sponsors, but never met them. "She stood the first couple up— never showed," said Captain Tom Jurkowsky, an Annapolis spokesman. "The next couple, she never contacted."

Some of her officers began noting her difficulties. One described Zamora as a loner who seemed frequently "distracted." "She was not a model midshipman," said the official. "I think she had all the potential, but she was just meeting minimum requirements."

Diane and Jay seemed to click early on in their boot camp experience at Annapolis, in part because Diane needed him. Her parents and Jay's mother attended Parents' Weekend, August 9–11, and learned that the two had already become close. In fact, they admitted to their parents that they had been reprimanded by upperclassmen for fraternizing because he was caught sitting on the edge of Diane's bed at night in Bancroft Hall.

"I got the very strong feeling that Diane's parents

felt the relationship between Diane and David had become an unhealthy one," recalled Jay's mother, Cheryl Guild.

During a lunch with Diane and her parents that weekend, Cheryl watched Diane having an animated phone conversation with David across the room and recalled Gloria leaning over to say, "I wish Diane had met Jay first."

Though they were loyal correspondents during boot camp, Diane soon began complaining that David was not answering her letters. At one point she told Jay she wanted to break off the engagement to Graham altogether; she asked Jay to become her boyfriend.

"She started dating me," Guild recalled. She also sent David an e-mail confessing that Jay had kissed her.

David responded, as Diane had perhaps hoped, with an e-mail message warning Jay to lay off. He even attempted to get Navy officials to investigate Jay for sexual harassment. David also wrote Diane letters begging her to remain faithful and reminding her of "what binds us together."

"Now you know how I felt," she messaged David back.

But it was already too late; Diane was breaking from the pressure of those bonds.

Halfway through the grueling boot-camp initiation, she confided to Jay that she and David had a secret "we'll take to the grave."

"She just came out and said he had cheated on her with this girl and she told him to kill her,"

Guild recalled. "I didn't want to believe her."

Zamora did not discuss the killing in great detail, Guild said, but the subject came up as many as fifteen times. "All she said is, she told him to do it and she saw him do it," Guild said.

"At first I thought she was telling me this to get attention," recalled Guild. "After that I would ask her—I'd try to ask her questions about why she would do something like that to get a feel as to whether she was joking or if she was telling the truth."

Gradually, Guild came to believe that Zamora "had the mentality to do it." But Guild never asked for details and, he said, she never volunteered any.

As he became increasingly friendly, he became increasingly protective. "The reason why I didn't turn her in," he would later say, was because "plebe summer is stressful for everybody" and they needed each other to make it through. "I was her squad leader and at that time she was having troubles and I would try to help her out. . . . She helped me a lot and I helped her and at that time we just—I felt loyal to her."

More remarkably, Guild thought, she expressed no remorse for the supposed murder, talking about it, he said, as if it were a rite of passage. "She said she would do it again," recalled Guild. "She only felt remorse for the girl's parents. She said it was part of her life that she had to go through."

The stress of his knowledge combined with the strain of plebe summer finally got to Guild. He began having trouble sleeping and concentrating. He even passed out in his dorm room. Physicians at the Academy's medical center said he had suffered a severe anxiety attack.

The roommates—Mandy Gotch, Jennifer Mc-Kearney and Diane Zamora—were a picture of America: McKearney from California, Zamora from Texas, Gotch from Maryland. And on this Saturday night, August 24, they shared a major accomplishment: they had survived plebe summer. Not without disquieting moments. McKearney, in fact, was new to this large suite in Bancroft Hall, joining Gotch and Zamora just the week before, after a roommate keeled over dead. Natural causes was the preliminary ruling, but the school was investigating.

Gotch was lying on her "rack," in a secluded corner of the dorm room when McKearney and Zamora returned from their Saturday night "liberty." It was 1:30 in the morning and the girls talked as they got ready for bed. At first, Gotch just listened.

"I could hear Jen and Diane talking," she recalled. "They were talking about Diane's boyfriend David. Diane constantly talked about her boyfriend. Diane always said how close she and David were and how sometimes it was stressful."

McKearney and Zamora were doing most of the talking.

Later, in separate accounts, the two roommates remembered the rest of that night's conversation:

Gotch: Jen asked her some questions about David and Diane was telling her how David just took her in and allowed her to live with him when her parents got into some financial problems and she was living out of her car. . . . That her boyfriend gave her everything she had and was talking about how he took care of her when she had her car wreck and almost lost her hand. She was telling Jen how he helped her with her medicine and was just there for her.

McKearney: Diane said that one of the things that he had helped her through was the car accident she had. She was really depressed about the accident because she was afraid she was going to lose her hand. David made sure that Diane ate and that she couldn't overdose on drugs. Also, when her parents lost their house and cars, David took her in and clothed her and fed her and gave her money to spend at the malls, anything that she needed or wanted. He basically supported her.

Gotch: As the conversation continued, Jen was asking her questions about her and David and finally asked her, "Are you a virgin?" Diane replied no, things would be much easier if she had not had sex with David.

McKearney: She said that it was easy to give her virginity to David, her boyfriend, because she loved him so much, but that she wished she hadn't because it made everything worse.

Gotch: Diane kept saying that she loved him so much that if anyone touched him she would kill them. Jen and I just continued to talk with her, asking questions. You could tell by the way she was talking that there was something else that she wasn't telling us.

McKearney: We started asking Diane why she felt that it ruined everything. She said that her boyfriend had misused her trust with it. Diane started talking about how close she was with David, her boyfriend, because they had been through so much together. And that they held each other's futures in the palms of their hands.

Gotch: Diane said that if they wanted to, they could ruin each other's lives.

Finally Jen came out and just said, "Did you kill someone?" Diane sat there. She finally said, "I can just say that someone is dead because of me."

McKearney: We jokingly asked if they had killed someone. She just looked at me funny and said, "I didn't kill anyone, though let's just say that because of me, somebody's dead."

Gotch: We asked her questions and she started to dance around the issue, but the conversation continued to get weird.

McKearney: We pushed and prodded her to release more information so that she didn't feel pressured. So she then told us that one night David came home and he was really upset. When she asked him what was wrong, he said that he had slept with another girl. He said he didn't understand why he had and that he was thinking of Diane the whole time. David asked Diane what he could do to make it up to her and she said to kill the girl. David said OK.

Gotch: At one point Diane said, "If the Academy knew what David and I were, they would not let us in." We asked her why. I'm not sure if I am telling this in the order it happened, just as I am remembering it.

Diane told us that she and her boyfriend beat each other up. She showed us a scar on her knee, telling us that it was from one of their knife fights. On one occasion, she said David put a belt around her neck and tried to choke her. He had claw marks on his neck from where she tried to choke him to death. Diane felt that this was normal activity.

McKearney: Diane told us how they started taking it out on each other. Like David put his belt around her neck and tried to strangle her to death. (She made claw marks on him from where she tried to strangle him.) She showed us a scar from a knife fight.

Gotch: Diane told us that David had come to her house one night and he was upset. She asked him what was wrong. He broke down and told her that he had slept with another female. He asked Diane what he could do to make it up to her. He told her that the whole time that he was having sex with this girl—Diane never said any names— anyway, he was thinking why is he doing this because he loved Diane. Diane said that she was mad and began beating her head against the wall in an attempt to kill herself. Diane said she made David tell her everything in detail. She did not tell us details, only that she told him to make it up to her, he would have to kill the girl. Diane said, "I want you to kill her."

Gotch: Diane said that she was driving. David was in the passenger side. The girl was in the back seat crying. She finally asked them, "You're going to kill me, aren't you?" Diane said yes. I know that they shot her, maybe in her stomach.

She started to justify their action by telling us David came from a violent childhood, and gave examples like, "Oh, when he was seven or eight years old, he tried to drown a dog in the pool. He then put a noose around the dog's neck and left it to hang. When he returned later the dog was dead and he threw it into the backyard of the neighbor." Diane told us how David's mom stabbed him in the elbow with a fork when he put his elbows on the table.

McKearney: David called the girl and went over to her house. Then Diane picked them up in the

car, they drove her around and the girl kept bab-
bling, asking if they were going to kill her and
crying. And Diane told her yes, they were going
to kill her. The girl was in the back seat and
David was in the front in the shotgun seat. Diane
was driving. The girl was crying and saying,
"Y'all are really going to kill me?" and Diane
answered yes. David was the one that pulled the
trigger, but it wasn't an immediate death. Not a
fatal blow. Diane said that she remembered very
well how the girl was whimpering a lot.

Gotch: Diane said that she had enough hate in
her for the girl that it did not bother her.

McKearney: Diane said that it didn't really faze
her because she felt so much hate for the girl.
Because David couldn't deal with the situation
and Diane was so level-headed, she dragged the
body out of the car, into the field, and then
cleaned up the blood inside the car. The girl
wasn't dead, so they just left her. Diane wanted
to weight down the body and throw it in the river,
but David couldn't handle it.

Gotch: Diane told me that her best friend and
her parents know that she killed the girl. Her parents told her that she should just pray and know
that next time she asked for something, she really
has to want it. Diane told us that she had also
told Midshipman 4/C Jay Guild about the murder.

*McKearney: Diane said that she saw the girl's
parents at the funeral and how she felt bad for
them, but that if she was in the same situation,
she would do it again. Diane also said that her
own parents know about this and her best friend
does too.*

*Gotch: We asked her if she was sorry for what
she had done. She said that the girl was pretty
and for that reason she was sorry. She said,
"Well, I guess I hated her so much, I would do
it again."*

By the time the young women finished their
amazing conversation, it was past three in the morning. But Gotch and McKearney couldn't sleep. "I
was afraid that Diane was going to hurt me," recalled Gotch.

But both women were incredulous about Diane's
story. "I thought at one point she might be making
it up and I wanted to get her some help," Mc-
Kearney later said. "But people just don't make stories up like that."

The two women felt compelled to tell someone
and, the next day, confided what they had heard to
an Academy chaplain. They were immediately
moved to other rooms, while the chaplain told the
school attorney Lieutenant Commander Patrick Mc-
Carthy, who talked to Zamora. Though she claimed
that she was just telling her roommates some Texas
tales, McCarthy was concerned enough to decide to
make some calls.

In what amounted to searching for a needle in a haystack, McCarthy began calling law enforcement agencies in the Fort Worth area. "We called the Tarrant County morgue, we called the Tarrant County prosecutor's office, we called the city of Dallas, we called the Fort Worth police department, we called the Tarrant County sheriff. We called all over. We didn't stop," McCarthy recalled. "We didn't just accept the standard answer, which was, 'Hey, this is a big state—unless you've got the name of the deceased, forget it.' "

McCarthy stumbled onto some good luck when he discovered that Zamora had listed a "temporary address" in Mansfield, Texas, on a personnel form.

Within a few hours he had made contact with Sergeant Julie Bain of the Mansfield police department. Bain told McCarthy about Adrianne Jones.

"It was kind of out of the blue," Bain recalled. "The Naval Academy called to see if any of the information they had in Annapolis was factual."

After the enormous number of dead-ends that she and other members of the team had pursued during the previous nine months, Bain was "skeptical." But it sounded good enough for her to call colleagues in Grand Prairie.

Grand Prairie detectives were dumbfounded by Bain's news. Sergeant Sager immediately called McCarthy in Annapolis to question him for himself. "I wanted to make sure this wasn't just some kid mouthing off," Sager recalled. "And McCarthy kept encouraging me to send someone out before the Navy closed the door on it. He was going to take care of making sure we had a chance to talk to her about it—but Navy brass was going to find out about it soon and then there would be no more talking."

Sager drove to Lieutenant Don Sherman's house to get permission to send someone to Annapolis.

"He says, 'There's no money for it. You guys aren't going anywhere,'" Sager recalled. "And then he says, 'If you solve this on somebody else, you will give McMillen a blank check.'"

Sager had been with the Grand Prairie police department long enough to know that politics sometimes influenced the decision-making process. "They know that as long as the case is unsolved, Bryan McMillen lives with this cloud over his head," said Sager. "And as long as he has the cloud over his head, he can't sue for false imprisonment."

Sager huddled with his deputies. Sherman had left him a way out by saying they couldn't go because of funds. Investigators decided they'd pay their own way to Annapolis. "I say, 'Look guys, I ain't got 600 bucks to spend on an airplane ticket, but we are going to go.'"

They managed to find round-trip tickets for $200 each and Sager called Sherman. "I said, 'Hey, Lieutenant, we got the tickets. We're paying for it ourselves. We just need permission to leave town.'"

Sherman agreed. Eventually, four investigators— three from Grand Prairie and Julie Bain from Mansfield—flew to Annapolis and the city of Grand Prairie paid.

Friday night Diane Zamora was pulled from the Academy's first football pep rally of the season and escorted to the main administration building, into an office where a group of Naval officials and plainclothes men and women waited, somber-faced.

The latter group introduced themselves as detectives from the Grand Prairie police department, then asked Diane about her recent confession to her roommates.

Diane immediately claimed to have made up the murder story to get attention, to make her seem tougher.

"She said at the time she was just lying for sympathy and to bring attention to herself," Sager recalled. "She admitted to making all the statements, but said they were simply comments made seeking sympathy or attention and that she did not murder anyone."

But police also interviewed Jay Guild after Zamora's roommates told them that he too knew about the killing. "I didn't believe Diane," he would later say. "I didn't believe there was even a murder until [police] started questioning me."

When they did arrive, Guild gave them an earful:

I don't know where to start. She told me basically everything about what she has done. I don't recall the girl's name. It was about four or five weeks ago. Ms. Zamora is in my squad. I was her squad leader and she was having a hard time. I helped her, and we began talking and then became friends. Sometimes we walked around the yard and one day we just started talking about cheating on boyfriends, girl-friends.

She told me that she was upset and what she had done was pretty bad. I asked her what she had done that was so bad. She told me that Mr. Graham, that is, her boyfriend David Graham, he is in the Air Force Academy, had cheated on her. He had been with a girl that he knew from school, they were on the same cross-country track team and he had a class with her.

Mr. Graham and Ms. Zamora had been dating and then after a track meet he went and visited this girl. He had sex with her at that time. Mr. Graham did not tell Ms. Zamora about it for a week or two. When Mr. Graham told Ms. Zamora, she was upset and told Mr. Graham to kill the girl. Mr. Graham called the girl up and asked her to meet him in a field out in the woods, and she apparently did.

From what I got from Ms. Zamora, they were in Mr. Graham's truck. She stayed in the truck and he shot her in a field. At first I thought this may be a bunch of crap, but after a while I believed her. She was always consistent in her story and why she wanted it done. We have talked about this on at least ten occasions.

Ms. Zamora told me the reason she told him to do it was because she hated her. I know that he does not have this truck anymore because she crashed it. She has a picture of it in her room.

I believed that she was involved in this because one day while at the squad table my squad leader asked me if I believe in the death penalty. Someone had brought it up because you see, we have to read three articles from the newspaper and then talk about it. Anyway, I told her that I do believe in it.

Later Ms. Zamora asked me if I believe that she should die for what she had done. I asked her if she would do it again and she said yes. I have asked her several times during our conversations why she did it, and she told me that at the time she felt it had to be done and that she would do it again. I asked her if she would really do it again and she stated she would do it again. Ms. Zamora stated that she believed that the girl deserved it and that she knew he was dating Zamora.

Ms. Zamora led me to believe that he killed this girl with a handgun, because when he walked up to the girl he did not have anything in his hands. Ms. Zamora said that he walked up to her and pulled it out and shot her. The girl started to run. He shot her again. She did

*not say how many times. I know he sold some
of his guns to buy Ms. Zamora a ring a couple
of months before she came here. Ms. Zamora
has told me that he is a gun collector and went
to gun shows. Ms. Zamora told me that Mr.
Graham had taken Ms. Zamora out to shoot.
They shot rifles and handguns. She did not like
to shoot rifles.*

*Ms. Zamora told me that she made David a
promise that if she had cheated on him, she
would, she'd kill that person.*

*Ms. Zamora described this person as being
blond and that David did not know her well.
She was good-looking. Ms. Zamora said she
had never met her before. Ms. Zamora said she
felt bad for the family. That bothered her. She
doesn't feel sorry for the girl because she knew
that David belonged to her. She's going
through pain too! Ms. Zamora said that David
was the last person to talk to her. Mr. Graham
was said to have called her on the telephone
and asked her to meet him in a field and she
left the house right after.*

*I know that the police talked to Mr. Graham.
August 11, Parents' Weekend, David made
threats toward me, telling Ms. Zamora that he
was on the Air Force honor guard and they
were scheduled to come to the Naval Academy
in about a month. At that time he was going to*

*do me physical harm. I heard this myself as
she was talking to him on the phone. She said
David wanted to know if I could beat him in a
fist fight. About a week ago, she showed me a
letter from Mr. Graham, where in the corner
of the letter Mr. Graham asked her if she had
told me about what happened to the girl. That
is all I recall at this time. I swear that the
information given above is true and correct.*

On Saturday, August 31, less than two months
after she arrived, Diane Zamora was ordered to take
leave and driven to Baltimore–Washington International Airport by Annapolis officials so she could
fly home while the matter was pending. Without a
confession from Zamora, the Texas police had no
more reason to arrest the young cadet now than before. But they were excited by what their two days
of interviewing at Annapolis had revealed—and by
what Diane Zamora did when her plane landed in
Atlanta. She changed her ticket and flew on to Colorado Springs.

"The police were well aware that she might do
something like that," recalled Lieutenant McCarthy. "And they in fact were almost hopeful that she
would do it. It was something an innocent person
wouldn't do. But a guilty person would go to Colorado Springs. That's one reason they in fact did
not want to be on the same plane with her."

What Diane and David discussed in Colorado is
unknown. But the two did have their pictures taken;

he wearing his blue Air Force uniform, she her Navy dress whites. "In that one moment," wrote Skip Hollandsworth, "they looked at the camera with a nearly desperate look, as if they knew that this was their last time together—that the fairy tale was over."

"They knew the whole deal was blowing up on them," said one investigator on the case. "They had Sunday and Monday together to discuss everything they were going to do. They made a decision about what each of them was going to say."

When Jay Green called the phone number on the card from Grand Prairie Detective Dennis Clay, he thought it might have something to do with his work as a volunteer on the "weed and seed" unit (drugs) of the Fort Worth police department. Police matters. But Clay asked him, instead, if he had a friend named David Graham.

"Yes, sir," said Green.

Clay asked Green if he could answer a few questions about his friend.

As Green drove the dozen miles to Mansfield, he assumed this had something to do with a security clearance for Graham. As a military man, he was well aware of the procedures. But as soon as he had shaken hands with the detective and sat down at a desk in a small office at the Mansfield police department, Clay asked, "Are you familiar with the Adrianne Jones case?"

"No, sir," said Green. He hadn't known Jones

and hadn't paid any attention to the case. The girl's name, vague to him even at the time of the murder, had completely disappeared from his mind.

Clay reminded Green who Adrianne Jones was. Green then remembered the Tuesday night C.A.P. meeting when some of his friends from Mansfield were talking about the murder. Clay asked if Graham had ever mentioned Jones to him.

"No, sir," said Green.

"I bet you wonder what you're doing here," Clay said.

"Yes, sir, I do," said the teenager.

Clay then reminded Green about the night that Graham and Zamora had knocked on his window.

"That was the night Adrianne Jones was killed," said Clay.

Suddenly, Green knew what was up. His buddy was suspected of murder. But he didn't want to believe it. This was some sort of trick, a way of testing his loyalty to Graham, the strength of his friendship—after all, that night Graham had said, "This never happened"—or maybe it was to test his own worthiness to be a Marine. It was a military test.

Clay asked about Graham's use and knowledge of guns. And he patiently helped Green recall the details of the couple's visit that December 4 night, finally telling the youth about Zamora's confession to her roommates in Annapolis. Suddenly, Green knew this was no test; it was real life.

Police arrived at the Air Force Academy on Wednesday, September 4, just after Zamora left. At first Graham also denied that Zamora had meant anything she had told her roommates.

He even agreed to take—but failed, on Thursday—a polygraph test. Then cops told him that they had talked to Jay Green, who told them about David and Diane's late night visit. Finally, Air Force officers told the young cadet that he had a duty to tell the truth and, in the waning hours of September 5, David Graham confessed.

He typed most of the confession himself, in front of a word processor. It was a four-and-a-half-page narrative that would become the plot line for dozens of news stories, magazine articles, books and at least one movie—perhaps, even a trial.

With a number of local and military investigators waiting in the room, Graham tapped into the night, dragging the process on past midnight. He was asked to initial the top and bottom of each page as he finished.

When he was done, as one forensic psychologist would later say, it resembled a Danielle Steel novel.

It was November 4 and I was giving a friend a ride home late one night after returning from a cross-country meet in Lubbock, Texas. Adrianne surprised me by asking me to take some turns that I knew were out of the way. After being directed onto a dark path behind an old elementary school, I parked the car. The events that followed are not pleasing for me to relate as they go completely against the moral background I have grown to appreciate. There were sexual activities, short-lived and hardly appreciated. I did willingly concede to the girl in these actions, but I knew they were wrong. Never before had I particiated in anything so meaningless and painful, painful that is, because I was letting down the one person I had swore [sic] to be faithful to. These actions were immediately regretted. In an attempt to make them right, I confessed to my good friend Joseph hours later. I simply asked for him to listen, then forget. "If anyone ever tells Diane," I said, "it will be me." The month that followed was one of guilt and shame. I was always being told by Diane that our relationship was so perfect and pure.

The love we share would never be broken and no one would ever come between us. No one, that is, except that one girl that had stolen from us our purity. I can never hold anything from Diane, nor she from me. She knew in my eyes that something was wrong the moment I decided to confess. When I did tell her, I thought the very life in her had been torn away. She was angry, she was violent and she was broken. For at least an hour, she screamed sobs that I wouldn't have thought possible. It wasn't just jealousy. For Diane, she had been betrayed, deceived, and forgotten all in that one meaningless instant in November. The purity which she held so dear had been tainted *in that one unclean act. Diane had always held her virginity as one of her highest virtues. When we agreed to be married, she finally let her guard down long enough for our teenage hormones to kick in.*

When this precious relationship we had was damaged by my thoughtless actions, the only thing that could satisfy her womanly vengeance was the life of the one that had, for an instant, taken her place. Diane's parents had similar problems in their relationship. She knew her father had often cheated on her mother. Diane didn't want Adrianne to be the same woman for me that her father had in his affair. The request of Adrianne's life was not for a second taken lightly by me. I couldn't even believe she would ask that of me. Well Diane's beautiful eyes have always played the strings of my heart, effortlessly. I couldn't imagine life without her. Not for a second did I want to lose her. I didn't have any harsh feelings for Adrianne but no one could stand between me and Diane. I was totally in love with her and always will be. I regret it now, for never did I imagine the heartache it would cause my school, my friends, Adrianne's family, or even my community. I guess I just shut it all out of my mind in that instant when I convinced myself that Diane was even worth murder. After Diane gave me the ultimatum I thought long and hard about how to carry out the crime.

I was stupid but I was in love.

The plan was to call Adrianne and convince her to come out to my car. That worked. The plan was to drive her out near Joe Pool Lake. That worked. The plan was to (and this is not easy for me to confess) break her young neck and sink her to the bottom of the lake with the weights that ended up being hit into her head. That didn't work. Diane was hidden in the back of the car. It was late, about 00:30 hours on the morning of December 4, 1995. I realized to [sic] late that all those quick, painless snaps seen in the movies were just your usual Hollywood stunts. The quick and painless crime turned into something that basically scared the #$% out of Diane and I. We realized that it was either her or us and Diane struck her in the back of the head with one of the weights while I held her.

I could see in Diane's eyes that she was confused and scared. She was first acting out of passionate rage, but now she was fighting from instinct. Adrianne somehow crawled through the window and to our horror, ran off. I was panicky and just grabbed the Makarov 9 millimeter to follow. To our relief (at the time) she was too injured from the head wounds to

*go far. She ran into a nearby field and col-
lapsed. I wanted to just jump in and drive off.
We were both shaken and even surprised by
the nature of our actions. Neither Diane nor
myself were ever violent people. In that short
instant I knew I couldn't leave the key witness
to our crime alive. I just pointed and shot. I
was very confused and scared. I probably
looked like the perverbial [sic] headless
chicken running around the crime scene. I fired
again and ran to the car. Diane and I drove
off. The first things out of our mouths were, "I
love you" followed by Diane's, "We shouldn't
have done that, David." "Well, nice time to
tell me."*

*I just wanted it to be a dream. We took the
quickest route to I-20 where we decided to
head to a well-trusted friend's home. John
[Jay] Green did exactly as I suspected: allowed us through his window (the usual entrance place to his room), allowed us to clean
up and collect our wits and even loaned me a
pair of shorts. My clothing had blood stains on
them and we disposed of them in a dumpster
near Diane's house. We then went back to Diane's house where we cleaned out the car and
went to sleep by the fire. The next day we returned the weights to my house. Diane was in
shock. I was just scared. Neither one of us
knew why anymore we had just done that. The
following days at school were so mentally*

*tough they make my summer at the Air Force
Academy look like a walk in the park. Never
had I even imagined so much guilt. They announced it on the intercom. My friends talked
about it in the halls. Everywhere I turned
someone was crying or just staring in shock
for reasons I alone was the cause of. I saw
Adrianne's mother in the grocery stores. I read
articles of how her family was coping, in the
papers.*

*One thing in particular has haunted me con-
stantly for the past eight months. I read a quote
from Linda Jones in which she said, "I hope
that her killer is out there and he's just being
eaten up with guilt." When I read that I just
wanted it to all go away. I wanted to be able
to drive Adrianne back home, to go to sleep
and to wake up back on December 3 free to
make decisions all over again. Diane wanted
to go back also. For weeks her infatuation was
with just being able to go back before September 26 when she wrecked my truck and injured
her hand. She wanted to change that and she
wanted to keep me from going to Lubbock. Diane was constantly depressed from the guilt.
She was also scared that I would be arrested.
She used to worry herself sick in school over
me and have to call me as soon as school was
out to make sure I was OK. It didn't really
matter, however, what any police or detectives*

found. What happened was over. Adrianne was
gone, I was responsible and it wasn't going
away.

Graham was ushered from the confession room
to the base jail and put under a routine suicide
watch. He was not allowed back to his room. Air
Force personnel inventoried and boxed all his per-
sonal possessions, then turned them over to Grand
Prairie police.

Police asked if he knew where Diane Zamora
was.

"Her grandparents'," said Graham.

One down, one to go.

It was almost two in the morning when the three
police cars pulled up to the small brick ranch home
in an older development on the far reaches of Fort
Worth's southern border. There were no lights on
in the house.

This time, they left the SWAT team at home.
Sergeant Chuck Sager, who headed the homicide
unit, was there himself. And he brought Detective
Alan Patton along. Patton was one of the department's veterans, the cowboy cop who had parked
his cruiser in front of the murderous truck driver's
roaring 18-wheeler in 1982 and still wore the scars
from the resulting 100-foot flight through the air.

"I figure Patton's going to crash through the
door," recalled Sager. "So I'm there to put a leash
on him." In fact, Patton stayed in the car, to phone

the house, while Sager went to the door, flanked by
two younger detectives and two uniformed officers
from Fort Worth police department. They were
there for backup as well as quick visual identification. "So there's no misunderstanding about who's
coming in your house," Sager recalled. "Besides,
we already had one possible lawsuit on this case. I
didn't want another."

Sager banged hard on the door. "Police!"

After a few moments the door opened slightly
and a girl peeked out from behind it. She looked
like she had been asleep, a reassuring sign for the
officers; it meant they probably weren't expected.

"Police, ma'am," said Sager. "May we come in?
We have an arrest warrant for Diane Zamora."

The girl opened the door and the cops rushed in.
Guns drawn, flashlights shining left and right, two
cops went down a hallway to the right and two went
left, shouting, "Police!" The bedlam was inten-
tional; they needed to move fast, to surprise people,
but they also wanted to wake them to the fact that
it was the law. Sager, holding his 45-mm pistol
high, had never shot anyone in his 23 years as a
cop and he always figured it was because he had
the gun drawn; safer to look menacing than innocent, he moved straight toward a fold-out sofa in
the living room. A man and a woman were on the
bed, spooned together, asleep, but fully clothed.

Lights were now going on.

Sager saw Patton coming his way. The room was
also filling up with an assortment of adults and children stumbling out of bedrooms.

An older woman shouted at the young girl who had opened the front door.

"How'd they get in?"

"Well, I let 'em in," she said softly.

"Why'd you do that!" shouted the woman.

But Sager wasn't listening. "Diane Zamora?" he said, looking at the woman on the bed.

"Yeah," whispered the woman, blinking sleep from her eyes. She rolled over slowly, staring up at the crowd of men now standing over her.

"Cuff her!" shouted Patton. "Cuff her!"

Sager, a soft-spoken, grey-haired man in his fifties, standing 6' 2" and weighing 250 pounds, motioned to the other detectives to wait. In this crowd, he didn't want to risk a bait-and-switch. Loyalties in families, he knew, were strong, even on murder charges and he didn't want one of Diane's sisters or cousins getting a free ride to the police station while Diane slipped away.

"You have some I.D., ma'am?" he said politely but firmly.

Zamora fumbled with her purse at the side of the bed and pulled out a plastic card. Military I.D., thought Sager, looking at Zamora's Annapolis mug; you can't get any better than that. ("We never did find out who the guy on the bed with her was," recalled Sager. "At the time we didn't care. I still don't.")

"Now, cuff her," he said.

Patton led the 18-year-old Annapolis cadet to his car for the 20-minute drive to Grand Prairie. When told that David had written and signed a full confession, Diane unburdened herself as well. She cried. But it appeared to Patton that the tears of remorse were because she knew she would be separated from David Graham.

Police later searched Graham's house and found, as he said they would, two barbell handles and weights—ranging from 2.5 to 10 pounds—and, in the attic, a Russian-made 9-mm Makarov handgun wrapped in duct tape, with a magazine and one live round.

Adrianne Jones's killers had finally been found.

14

THE END OF THE DREAM

September 6, 1996.

I screamed at the top of my lungs, dropped the phone, busted out crying and got up and went to the bathroom and threw up for about a half-hour.

When Sarah Layton got up, she called her friend Joanna Christenson. But Joanna had already left for the football game. When Sarah caught up with her friend, Joanna was presenting colors at halftime.

She was in the middle of the field having a nervous breakdown. She got out there and cried through the whole thing.

When she got off the field, Joanna too collapsed in a heap sobbing.

What do you say? said Joanna. *One of your really good friends that you looked up to and admired and wanted to follow in his footsteps is now dressed up in orange and stuck in a jail cell? I don't believe that he did it. I'll probably never believe he did it.*

Said Sarah: *I don't think it matters that he signed a confession, because I honestly think that if Zamora had that much power over him to get him to even be there or even think about it, there's no tell-*

*ing how she could get him to cover for her. David
would cover for anything. He was totally gaga over
her.*

Said Mike Grubbs: *He is awesome—I can't believe he would do something like that. It's definitely
not him.*

Lorena Jordan: *I remember being flabbergasted
when I heard Diane had been arrested. I was sitting
in my car, waiting to pick up my children from
school, when I heard the news on the radio. I'm
glad I wasn't driving because I think I would have
had an accident. I kept saying, "This can't be the
same Diane Zamora. There must be some mistake."*

Mattie Crisman: *I have known David all his life.
I never knew of anything he did wrong. . . . Last
night we could hardly go to sleep. Went to bed and
got to talking about it and you just couldn't hardly
believe that it happened.*

Mike Santos: *What people are reading in the papers and hearing on the news about [Diane] is exactly the opposite of the kind of person she really
is. This is all such a shock. It just doesn't make any
sense. Diane worked so hard to get where she was.*

Adrianne Jones's death had slipped slowly from
the front pages of the papers to anniversary feature
status. The murder had, over the months, become a
kind of dull throb in a slightly used part of the body
politic. The investigation had been for a few months
like a Mack truck storming down the center of the
highway, and was now a tiny vehicle on the shoul-
der of the road—like the sign that Linda Jones in-

stalled in the Winn-Dixie parking lot. The murder was there, unchanged, a reminder so fixed that it was of the landscape. The town was almost used to her death, to its unanswered questions and unsolved mysteries. Everything had been so quiet that people were kind of used to thinking that this was a crime without a culprit. It was and would be unrequited, unavenged. It would simply be, like Linda Jones's sign, a rough spot on the side of the road.

And that is where the case was on the morning of September 6, 1996, when the news wires awoke and the phone lines began buzzing.

In fact, it would be two thousand miles away, in Baltimore, that the story would first break. The *Baltimore Sun* had already moved to newsstands and homes throughout the east coast with a front-page story that would shock the small town of Mansfield, Texas.

"A U.S. Naval Academy freshman was placed on leave Saturday after she was questioned by Texas police in connection with a homicide that occurred before her arrival this summer in Annapolis, academy officials and Navy sources said." The story also noted that she had implicated her boyfriend, an Air Force Academy cadet.

The Academy was tightlipped about the details, however. "Law enforcement officials interviewed a midshipman regarding knowledge of an alleged incident," said a spokesman in a written statement. "The midshipman is presently on leave out of the area at home and will be until such time as the matter is resolved," said Jurkowsky. "The investigation is ongoing and no charges have been filed against any midshipman pertaining to the matter.''

The Air Force was no more forthcoming, admitting only that police from Grand Prairie, Texas had interviewed a freshman male cadet ''regarding possible knowledge of the incident.''

And, despite an official ''no comment'' from Deputy Chief Brad Geary of the Grand Prairie police department, the Baltimore reporters were able to piece together enough of the story from background sources to know that the Texas cops were interested in the Adrianne Jones murder. And though they managed to interview a friend of Adrianne's, she said she hadn't heard of the midshipman.

At 6:02 that morning—5:02 in Mansfield—the Associated Press put the story on its national wire:

> *A first-year female midshipman at the U.S. Naval Academy was placed on leave after being questioned by Texas police about a homicide last December, academy officials said. The 18-year-old woman's name was not released and academy officials refused to give any details of the case or say why the midshipman was questioned. They confirmed she was placed on leave last Saturday.*

Mansfield Police Chief John Young called a press conference. ''On Friday, September 6, Diane Zamora and David Graham were taken into custody'' for the murder of Adrianne Jones, said Young. ''Investigators from the Mansfield and Grand Prairie police departments also recovered a 9-mm Makarov handgun at the Graham residence.''

Officials from Mansfield High School were visibly shaken as they gathered at another hastily called meeting for the press. Principal Jerry Kirby, sitting next to school superintendent Vernon Newsom and school counselor Susi Park, kept shaking his head.

"I think all of us are surprised," he said. "It's really hard to make any comment because it really hasn't sunken in. David was never a discipline problem."

The school administrators all knew Graham, could tick off his honors and awards, including a National Merit Scholar commendation and an ROTC leadership recognition medal. Kirby promised, yet again, that additional counselors would be called in to help students who needed it.

"I can't speculate how this is going to end," said Kirby.

"I think everyone's in shock right now and doesn't feel like talking," Crowley principal Bill Johnson said after emerging from a meeting with the school's teachers.

Gradually, during the day, accounts about the "confessions" began to leak. Grand Prairie cops, exultant at having finally solved the case, were more than happy to speak.

One officer said it was a story of "love, jealousy and retribution." Another said it was "love, passion and anger."

If nothing else, it was, as *Fort Worth Star* senior writer Tim Madigan wrote, "one of the more remarkable confessions in recent memory."

After initially denying involvement in Jones's death, they said, Graham had written and signed a confession. In it he admitted to a "one-time intimate encounter" with Jones that "fed a jealous relationship," said an anonymous police officer.

The motive was clear, said Chuck Sager: "Guilt, passion and anger." The murder "was his penance," Sager said. But "they were both there and they both participated."

"When I heard who did it, you're thinking, 'The Air Force Academy and Naval Academy?' " said Frank Rogen, a school district policeman. "We're talking about people protecting the United States of America."

Linda Jones had her own press conference. "I don't know him," she said of Graham. "But I can tell you that three young lives—not just Adrianne's—have been taken because of senseless violence."

Instead of relief, Jones's despair and outrage was rekindled.

"These are not stupid kids," she said of Graham and Zamora. "These are scholastic achievers. They destroyed Adrianne's life. They destroyed their own lives. They no longer have careers. They could have had prestigious careers, they could have gotten married and had children of their own. That's not going to happen now. . . . I think it's so stupid. It's beyond belief. My daughter is dead because of somebody being so jealous. It's bizarre. It's sad that all of these lives have been destroyed for no reason."

Jones reserved her sympathies for Graham's and Zamora's parents. "I feel for the parents," she said. "I really do. Almost 10 months ago to the day I was saying, 'No, no, no, not my child.' Now they are saying that."

"These were two kids who had the world by a string," said Brad Geary, Grand Prairie's deputy police chief. "Why would they do something like that?"

Bill Jones was in no mood for felicitous understandings. "They manipulated, ambushed and murdered Adrianne," he said the day after Graham and Zamora were arrested. "They were two predators out there."

The day after the arrest, the morning paper lay on the ground in front of 103 Cedar Street well past noon. Still in its clear plastic wrapper, the headline was partly visible, "Two Honor Students . . ."

This is not how Jerry Graham thought it would end with his fair-haired son. He and his separated wife, who now lived in Houston, would disappear behind shuttered windows to be alone with their horror.

Thanks to David's sister, the family retained well-known Houston attorney Dan Cogdell. And Cogdell immediately dispatched his associate, Robert Swofford, to Colorado. Janice Graham also flew to Colorado Springs, on Sunday, and visited David. But she didn't go to court with her son the following day.

"They are just shattered," Cogdell told the *Dal-*

las Morning News about Graham's family, wasting no time taking calls from the press. "This kid is a straight-A, honor-roll, pick-of-the-litter kid who has never done anything wrong in his life. Now, he's accused of murder."

As for Graham himself, "He is scared to death," said Cogdell.

"Grand Prairie claims he was the shooter—he was not," said Cogdell. "He never intended to kill the girl, nor did he intend to have anyone else kill her." While admitting that his client was present when Jones was killed, he accused police of constructing a statement for Graham. It was clear to Cogdell that Graham's confession would be the lynchpin of any case against his client. Everything the attorney said was meant to undermine the power of that statement.

Cogdell said he would not oppose Graham's extradition to Texas. "We want to get him back to Texas as quickly as we can," Cogdell said. "There's no utility in trying to hide him away in Colorado. . . . He's an 18-year-old kid who is facing a murder charge. He's scared to death."

Rob Swofford was there when the lanky young Air Force cadet made the first court appearance of his life. He was marched into a large room, with a couple dozen suspected criminals, all wearing bright orange, jail-issue jumpsuits—like the ones Timothy McVeigh, suspected Oklahoma City bomber, and Theodore Kaczynski, the Unabomber suspect, wore at their initial federal proceedings. In fact, the lanky Graham, with his short, blond military haircut, resembled McVeigh. He tried to shield his face from the crowd of reporters watching him from an adjoining glass-enclosed room while he talked with a fellow inmate.

It was a shocking transformation for the teenager who had just a few days before been wearing an Air Force blue uniform, marching in an honor guard on the campus of one of the nation's premier military academies.

When it was his turn, Graham stood and addressed District Judge Willis Kulb, whose face was on a television monitor at the front of the room. Kulb was actually in a courtroom ten miles away, conducting the hearing via video monitor. He asked Graham if he understood his rights.

"Yes, sir," said Graham in a soft, barely audible voice, his hands clasped tightly together in front of him. Kulb then asked Graham to sign the papers that would acknowledge his agreement to be sent back to Texas for trial. Since Kulb couldn't see Graham—it was only one-way video—he asked the suspect to raise his right hand and swear that he had read the waiver of extradition and signed it "willingly and intentionally."

"I swear," said Graham.

The importance of Graham's "confession" took on new meaning when a copy of it was leaked to the *Dallas Morning News.* "This guy gave it up because they were so scared of being finger-pointed on this," said one investigator, fingering a Grand Prairie police official as the source of the leaked confession. "They didn't want any more bad publicity or have anyone going, 'Here you go again. You have no evidence and you're railroading this kid.' It was already starting, with Graham's mother and this Houston attorney screaming about what the police were doing to this poor kid. The next day is when you saw the confession come out."

Apprised of the paper's intention to publish excerpts, attorney Cogdell called a preemptive press conference and again lashed out at the police. "The statement was taken after 30 hours' worth of interrogation, after he was denied counsel, promised that he was better off without a lawyer, promised if he gave a statement he would receive probation and threatened with capital murder if he did not make a statement," he said. "Not surprisingly, [the statement] is consistent with what law enforcement wants the statement to contain."

Cogdell refused to say what he thought really happened, but did admit that Zamora had visited Graham in Colorado Springs just before her arrest. "They had an opportunity to discuss who would take the blame," he said, laying more of the groundwork for doubts about what would be a key piece of evidence in any subsequent trial: his client's "confession."

"One, you've got police, who have already had a track record in this case of charging an innocent person with the crime, continuing to investigate it," Cogdell said, referring to the arrest and release of Bryan McMillen earlier that year. "Two, you have a love-triangle situation where it is more than consistent with the expectation that he may be perhaps covering for his lover or his girlfriend," he said. "And three, you've got the usual problems involved in any statement-taking about police misinterpreting what you have to say."

Cogdell said that David wrote the confession to cover for Diane.

In any case, he continued, "Graham never intended to kill the girl. Nor did he intend to have anyone else kill her." Graham concocted the confession to protect Zamora, he said.

But almost as soon as Cogdell had raced out of the gate, he was reined in. Less than a week after Graham's arrest, Cogdell announced, "Janice Graham gave me this directive yesterday: 'I want justice for my son, but I do not want that at the expense of injustice to others. I do not want the Zamora family dragged through the mud. She, Diane, was welcome in my house.'" Cogdell admitted, "It's never happened to me," and said, "Now, whether I can follow that advice is an open question."

"My position is I'm not going to demonize Diane Zamora and I'm not going to say anything negative about the Jones girl," Cogdell would later say. "I'm not going to bring anybody down. If there comes a time that I have to say some things about Diane Zamora, I'm going to do that in a courtroom, not the press."

Cogdell even expressed sympathy for Zamora's family, evidencing his skills at sophistry. "The natural reaction," he said of Diane, "is to try and shift the blame or say that it's someone else's fault."

*   *   *

News of the arrests left administrators and students at both high school campuses stunned.

The story was big enough for the *Fort Worth Star Telegram* to fly reporters to Annapolis and Colorado Springs and for the *Baltimore Sun* to send one of its scribes to Mansfield.

Zamora quickly became the first Naval cadet ever arrested for murder—though no one could be sure of that fact. It was the same for Graham at the Air Force Academy.

"They seemed to be what represented the best, but unfortunately at this turn, you find out otherwise," said Charlotte Crowe, a spokeswoman for the Civil Air Patrol's headquarters at Maxwell Air Force Base in Montgomery, Alabama. "It's disturbing."

Local experts weighed in with psychological explanations of why two high-achieving teenagers would do such a thing.

"Their success may have ballooned the confidence they had in themselves to the point that they felt far superior to anyone who might try to detect them," said Dr. Jaye Crowder, assistant professor of psychiatry at the University of Texas Southwestern Medical Center in Dallas.

Being a superachiever does not mean someone automatically has a conscience, said Ray Eve, a sociology professor at the University of Texas at Arlington.

"Just because a person has very high grades and

looks like a model citizen does not always indicate that they are a fine human being," he said. "Occasionally, bright people decide that the rules are for ordinary people and they're above that."

Dr. Laura King, a Southern Methodist University assistant psychology professor, said that the case proved just how difficult it is to know what people are capable of and illustrated that the image many people have of criminals as violent individuals is not always accurate.

"People tend to think of criminals as being violent or aggressive, poor, troubled individuals with low self esteem and hatred of themselves," she said. "It may not be that at all. It may be an inflated sense of their own importance that leads people to do these things."

In some cases, extremely bright people who appear to be socially outstanding are extremely manipulative, Eve said. In other cases, a lifetime of pressure to excel can backfire and lead to violence.

Crowder believed that someone who is dependent on another can react violently to the fear of a breakup. A personality disorder could lead someone to become desperate to hold on to a relationship.

"He may have come to equate happiness with being with her," Crowder said. "And he may have felt desperate to hang on to that relationship."

Henry Tatum, associate editor of the *Dallas Morning News* editorial page, began his September 18 article, "The headline is sure to be nominated for understatement of the year: 'Puzzling Case.

Teenagers accused in slaying of Mansfield girl don't fit common criminal profiles, experts say.'

"Mr. Graham's angst-ridden confession to the crime has made the murder of the teenage girl in December all the more sickening," said Tatum.

Tatum believed the larger question was this: "How can young people today have so little regard for a human life that they would take it in order to prove a point?"

The *Fort Worth Star Telegram* felt strongly enough about the case to run a lengthy editorial.

In the news business this is a huge story for very human reasons: because these are our neighbors' children; because of the youth of Jones and the mystery of the popular scholar–athlete's violent demise; because the pair in custody are engaged to be married; and because Graham and Zamora are bright, successful young people just beginning their first year of study at the Air Force and Naval Academies, respectively.

If the police are right, this is a story of youthful pain and misguided passion that begat violence and death. It will attract much media attention precisely because it assaults our values at so many levels. It has the power to move us all because it contains such mystery, because it conjures so many questions and because the questions are the kind that strike so close to the heart . . .

*Is it possible that two students so blessed could
be so wrong?*

*Is it possible that young people so committed
to national service and, presumably, to national values could be connected to so terrible
an event?*

*Is it possible that someone with a murder story
to tell can be accepted at the nation's exclusive
military academies?*

*Is it possible—and this is a troubling question
that police are pursuing—that others knew the
details of this murder and kept silent?*

*Is it possible that, in this day and time, such
things can happen here among us? Is there
anything that the rest of us can do about them?*

*Such questions numb the mind and break the
heart, and leave us searching in the darkness
for meaning.*

These were the questions, the paper guessed cor-
rectly, that many people had. And inadvertently perhaps, the editorial predicted the media onslaught
that would come.

Within two days of the arrests of Zamora and
Graham, the Mansfield school district had received
dozens of calls from national reporters, including

Hard Copy, *Inside Edition*, *Day and Date*, *The Montel Williams Show*, *People* magazine, *The New York Times*, the *Baltimore Sun* and the *Washington Post*.

"It's the type of story that may sadden local residents but attracts readers and television viewers, said Jan Murray, a spokeswoman for Kingworld Productions, which produced the syndicated television show *Inside Edition*. "If all the facts are true, it's a great story about the test of commitment and passion and greed—all those elements our audience seems to really like."

"What makes it interesting is the cadets," said Matthew Bracks of *Day and Date*.

The release of Graham's confession to the *Dallas Morning News* only made the stampede more intense. It was all there. Youth, love, honor and, the most important ingredient of all, murder. For a media industry that had saturated—and amply satiated—the country with the sordid O. J. Simpson murder case, this was fresh; everything that O. J. and Johnny Cochran and Mark Fuhrman weren't. Instead of a jaded city, this was a killing that "shocked two small towns"; instead of mansions and limos, high-priced drugs, sex and domestic abuse, these were "teenagers [who were] academic and athletic standouts" only recently "nominated for their [service] commissions by their congressmen."

Adrianne Jones had been dead for ten months—with barely a word about the case from any media outlet outside of Texas. But now that the case had, in the words of *The New York Times,* "embroiled two of the nation's service academies," it was as if, instead of "A Tale of Love and Murder," the headline in the *Times* read, "Gentlemen, Start Your Engines!"

In the middle of the press onslaught Linda Jones composed a letter to the editor of the *Mansfield News-Mirror,* but it was meant for her fellow Mansfield citizens. It expressed both her thanks for the arrests—and her exasperation over what her daughter, in death, was being subjected to.

I want to say the Jones family is very glad to know who is "allegedly" responsible in Adrianne's death. We also are saddened by the absolutely strange and bizarre twists this case has gone, and will continue to move, through. . . .

One thing I am sorry about is the over- whelming news-media blitz. Please know we are not any happier about this than you all are. A candlelight ceremony will be held soon for the city of Mansfield, our friends and families to help with closure. Let's now gather together and strengthen our bonds of community.

We thank everyone! All of you . . . more than you know. We are lifted in prayer. So are you.
                                        Linda Jones

P.S. Good-bye for now, Adrianne Jones. In another time . . . In another place . . .

She was even more forthright about her feelings with a Fort Worth reporter, angrily denouncing suggestions that her daughter was some kind of "sleeparound."

"I'm tired of hearing that. I want it to quit," she said.

"If it would have been two punks, do you think it would have made this much media? I don't enjoy the national spotlight. It's just their way of keeping their ratings up. This flash-in-the-pan thing will be over soon enough."

Where was all the media during those long months after the murder?

"Ever since her August 25 revelation to her roommates—and the resulting formal confessions to police—their admirers at the service academies and the Fort Worth suburbs where they lived have been unable to believe that these two could behave like [characters in] *Natural Born Killers,*" wrote Mark Thompson of *Time* magazine.

"There aren't too many accomplished people," said Republican Pete Geren, a Democrat from Texas, who nominated Zamora for her Naval Academy appointment, "able to hide such dark sides."

"That's exactly what's so haunting about this case," wrote Thompson. "Nothing in their background suggests a capacity for murder."

"A year ago, all I wanted to know was who killed her and why," recalled Lee Ann Burke, the cross-country coach who knew both Jones and Graham. "Now that we know, it doesn't seem to help."

"It's not any easier [knowing that David was arrested]," said Sarah Layton. "It gets worse. Because now, it's like one minute you're crying, and the next minute you're arguing that he had nothing to do with it. And you're so confused; you don't know why it's going on."

"What infuriates me the most," Jeff Lackey told Ellise Pierce, "is that while we're here struggling in school to keep our sanity, he [Graham] was sitting next to us and walking around us. And none of us had the slightest clue that it could've been him. He put us all through so much pain, and I hope he saw it and realized that he was the cause of it."

There was no confusion on the part of Bill Jones. Watching a television report on the murder not long after the arrests of Graham and Zamora, he shouted at the set, "Why don't you say what he really is? He's a spineless little shit who could be manipulated so dramatically by a girl with so much passionate jealousy. What kind of a spineless asshole are you?"

"It's pointless," said Linda Jones about the debate over who *actually* pulled the trigger. "Absolutely pointless! So it's—I don't understand why kids today are the way they are. I cannot comprehend it. . . . It's just stupid. There's no reason for it.

And now her life is gone, and these other people's lives are gone."

"These were two intelligent kids," said Bill. "Nobody seems to argue that. But these kids were never taught consequences. If these kids would have considered consequences, three months, six months, nine months down the road, there is no doubt in my mind they would not have done this."

People magazine arrived on newsstands on October 14—Adrianne Jones was on the cover. For stars and starlets, this was one of the most coveted publicity placements in the world. Adrianne, her studio picture run as large as any movie star on the cover, was as pretty as most of them. It was a picture Adrianne herself had never seen. "It was supposed to be her Christmas present," said Linda Jones.

Ellise Pierce, who did some reporting for *People,* wrote a lengthy story about the effect of the murder on Mansfield's teenagers for the *Dallas Observer.* It was a cover story for the tabloid weekly, called "Love is a Killer," and it explored the topography of the murder with precision.

"This seemingly nonsensical talk of young love gone amok touches on all the anxieties of Mansfield youths. Not quite adults, they find themselves dealing with adult problems: sexual jealousy, pressures to achieve, violence. They flaunt their sexual freedom, yet talk about beating each other up for infidelities, and using guns to settle disagreements.

"The seemingly cold-blooded killing of Adrianne

Jones has left many people wondering how two kids with so much promise could commit such a horrifying crime. But while Mansfield teens say they're shocked and angered by the discovery that one of their own classmates is accused of the murder, the overall impression they leave is one of emotional numbness.

"Listening to their detached, hollow voices is both bleak and surreal—almost as haunting as Adrianne Jones's murder itself."

After the "confession" was released, there were new theories about what would have motivated two bright young people to kill someone. Now, the "love triangle" hypothesis had—according to Graham's confession, at any rate—to be considered.

"This is a very strange situation," said Barrie Levy, a California psychotherapist and editor of *Dating Violence: Young Women in Danger.* "One part of being an adolescent is that things can be very dramatic and very intense. But that rarely leads to murder. That's no more typical of teens than of anyone else."

"This reads like Danielle Steel confesses to murder," Sharri Julian, a forensic psychologist, told the *Houston Chronicle.* "You can almost see the Duke riding up on his white horse to save the damsel."

Richard Hawkins, a sociology professor at Southern Methodist University, saw the crime as morality gone awry. "To argue that this was an immoral killing is ridiculous—it was a hyper-moral killing," Mr. Hawkins said, pointing to the teenagers' emphasis on fidelity and trust. "This is one of those times when a social good fosters a social bad."

And Hawkins suggested that "We are not teaching our youths how to make moral judgments." "They know the rules, but they don't know how to apply them. People have to learn what the Ten Commandments are and what the moral code is, but they also need to know what the appropriate response is when indiscretions occur."

"My opinion is just that, an opinion," said Julian. "I haven't examined either of these kids, but it's clear that this whole case is about sex."

Barri Rosenbluth, a Texas social worker and director of the Teen Dating Violence Project in Austin, agreed. "It's exaggerated, but it's not so different from what I see every day. . . . The difficulty young people have with the intensity of their relationships, their feelings of jealousy and anger."

"All emotions are exaggerated in adolescence," Dr. Jonas R. Rappeport, a forensic psychiatrist told the *Baltimore Sun,* "because adolescents don't have a lot of experience with them." Teens tend to "see things more in black and white," he said.

"It's also about '*folie à deux*' (a shared pathological disorder)," said Julian. "You've got two people who, individually, would probably never do anything like this, but they become so intertwined with one another that they form a third person. They're bright, intellectual people who both probably perceive of themselves as highly moral, but then they come together. . . . Somehow, out there in the cosmos, these two celestial bodies collide and this is what they produce.''

"Experts say youth violence has risen in recent years for a variety of reasons,'' wrote Michael Saul and Barbara Kessler in the *Dallas Morning News.* "The loosening of community ties, broken families, distances between relatives and the media's glamorization of violence. As a result, many teens don't know how to control or vent their emotions.''

They quoted Jane Grady, assistant director of the Center for the Study and Prevention of Violence at the University of Colorado in Boulder. "They're acting it out to the extreme instead of possibly considering the outcome,'' she said. "They're just acting out on the extreme emotions they feel.''

Said Dr. Stewart Keller, assistant professor of psychiatry and human behavior at the University of North Texas Health Science Center at Fort Worth: "Their lives were in a state of flux and they didn't want to lose the one constant. Possibly the idea of losing all that, at least for him, was too much. . . . What is so unusual in this case is the background that these kids come from tends to make us say, 'Not these kids,' '' he said. "In this case, it's like you show me that you don't care about me. To prove that you do, you've got to do something extreme. This is pretty extreme.''

Baltimore Sun journalists Tom Bowman, JoAnna Daemmrich and Scott Shane found it ironic that the plaque in front of the tree planted in Adrianne's honor at Mansfield High School read "Strength, Unity, Courage."

Graham and Zamora, they wrote, "killed . . . in the name of virtues like those attributed to their victim. In the distorted vision that grew from their intense relationship, they were reestablishing their own unity, which had been threatened by Graham's one-time sexual indiscretion with 16-year-old Adrianne. In their mirror world, victim and villains changed places, and they were demonstrating strength and courage by taking swift action to right an intolerable wrong."

Barrie Levy guessed that there was something in the Zamora–Graham relationship that no one really knew about.

Mansfield police decided to leave the sign in front of the Winn-Dixie parking lot offering a reward for tips about the murder of Jones. They hoped that someone could still shed some light on the bizarre case. They still wondered if, in this odd world, this might not be another *River's Edge,* a movie about a California murder that was known, it seemed, to every kid on the block—none of whom would step forward.

In fact, police knew about Mandy Gotch's haunting statement: "Diane told me that her best friend and her parents know that she killed the girl. Her parents told her that she should just pray and know that next time she asked for something, she really has to want it."

"The virtues of their prayer groups and gun

shows, athletic contests and close-order military drill,'' wrote Tom Bowman of the *Baltimore Sun*, ''were perverted to provide the means and the motive to kill.''

15

LOVE'S LAST LIES

For a time, it seemed, Diane had less trouble adjusting to prison life than to Naval Academy life. After trading in her plebe whiteworks for prison-issue jumpsuit, she moved from a cozy dorm room at Bancroft Hall to a small cell in the two-story Grand Prairie jail.

She was quick to start exercising, running in place, and doing sit-ups and push-ups. Her father called once to say his daughter complained of being cold and asked if jailers could bring her more blankets. They complied. Though Grand Prairie police reported that she seemed remorseful, they said that her biggest concern was that she would be separated from Graham.

When she was transferred to the modern Tarrant County Justice Center in Fort Worth, Diane was whisked to a solitary confinement unit that consisted of a three-cell pod on the fifth floor. Though isolated from other prisoners, she was able to watch T.V. and could begin to follow the coverage her case was receiving. Even then, however, she spent

most of her time in her single cell exercising and
writing letters.

The family contacted Houston attorney Richard
"Racehorse" Haynes, who had twice successfully
defended Fort Worth millionaire Cullen Davis. But
Haynes said no, recommending Fort Worth attorney
John Linebarger.

On Tuesday, September 10, Linebarger announced that he would be representing Zamora, and
the next day held a press conference at the Tarrant
County Justice Center. He described his client as in
a "state of bewilderment and shock."

But, said Linebarger, "She's real calm for someone her age in these circumstances."

Linebarger, like Dan Cogdell, was quick to defend his client against the presumption of guilt.
"Diane, to my satisfaction, has not been proven
guilty of anything," he said. "There's no way to
plead other than not guilty. . . . I haven't ruled anything out, but we're certainly not going to enter a
plea of guilty under any circumstances."

Asked whether Zamora would testify against Graham, Linebarger, who claimed not to have seen any
"confession," said, "Each case rises and falls on
its own facts. If they're pitted against each other,
they are. And if they're not, they're not. But this is
not a team effort, at least it isn't right now."

What did concern Linebarger was that, "All she
wants to know is when she can see [David] or talk
to him."

Diane was put in a solitary cell, continued to do

push-ups and sit-ups, read the Bible, but asked for a history book as well. She mostly kept to herself, except for singing a Christian hymn—"Faith"—to a prisoner who was crying for her children.

And, admitted her attorney, she was still talking constantly about David Graham. "One of her main concerns is seeing David and talking to him," said Linebarger. "When I tell her that is not going to happen, she says I should be able to fix it because I am an attorney."

Privately, Linebarger would tell associates he had never seen such an obsession between two people.

Like Linebarger, Cogdell was less than enthusiastic about linking the two suspects. And, a day after announcing Janice Graham's order not to attack Diane Zamora, Cogdell said, "If I think attacking the Zamora girl is the appropriate line of defense, I will do it. The defenses in my mind are inherently conflicting." Cogdell seemed to be letting Janice Graham know that his services on behalf of her son might come at Diane Zamora's expense.

But he did agree with Linebarger about one thing: the love his client had for the other suspect. "He is, as of last night, very much in love and very much concerned for Zamora," Mr. Cogdell said. "I am concerned that these two have almost a chemical need to be together right now."

Meanwhile the Tarrant County district attorney's office in Fort Worth received the case on September 10 and up to the plate stepped prosecutor Mike Parrish, a former Dallas cop.

Parrish said that the cases would be presented to a county grand jury, which would have 75 days to decide whether to indict Graham and Zamora. His office had ordered, for instance, that the gun found in Graham's house be test-fired so that the bullets could be compared with the one recovered from Jones's hair.

All the attorneys were predicting a trial within six to 12 months. But the strategies of the lawyers were complicated by the number of parties involved. Facing two defendants accused of the same crime, Parrish enjoyed a tactical advantage if he could successfully play one defendant off against the other. Offering Zamora a plea bargain in return for her testimony against Graham, for instance, would almost guarantee a conviction. It would offer Zamora, symbolically, a chance to do to Graham what he had done to her: betray.

Parrish had the option of filing capital murder charges against the defendants if the killing occurred in the course of "committing or attempting to commit kidnapping, burglary, robbery, aggravated sexual assault, arson or obstruction or retaliation."

Capital murder would allow him to seek the death penalty, which Texas had—and used. But, to get it, jurors had to unanimously agree that death was required. "In Texas, the jury has to answer that question unanimously yes," said Parrish, adding that other considerations include whether the defendants have a criminal history and whether the victim was a stranger. It didn't matter who fired the shots that

killed Jones, he pointed out. Each was equally responsible before the law.

"I think it would be almost impossible for them
to get the death penalty based upon their pristine
backgrounds and their bright promise for the future," said Michael Heiskell, a defense lawyer and
former federal prosecutor who had represented capital murder defendants. "It may not be that difficult
to get a capital murder conviction without the death
penalty, depending on the facts of the kidnapping.
But I think it would be a waste of time, energy and
resources to go for the death penalty in this case."

Parish eventually agreed. He charged the two
with capital murder, but would not seek capital punishment.

For the two honor students, going to jail presented
a host of questions not normally asked of murder suspects. Would Zamora receive an honorable discharge
from the Naval Academy? Her greatest "desire in
this world was to finish the Naval Academy and be
an astronaut," said Linebarger. (The Academy said
they were "removing" her from the school; Zamora
later "resigned.") The Air Force had stopped Graham's cadet stipend of $548 a month as soon as he
was put in "civilian confinement." And they were
offering a couple of options, according to Lieutenant
Colonel Doug McCoy. "Either he can resign or we
can disenroll him."

Said Linebarger: "You have two children who
I'd think would be the future leaders of America.
I've represented every type of case—these people

represent a unique group of the accused.''

Graham was flown to Texas on Monday, September 16, aboard a commercial airliner. Six armed policemen escorted the 18-year-old suspect to the American Airlines gate at the Colorado Springs airport for the hour-and-45-minute flight. Graham was dressed in a brown t-shirt and camouflage pants tucked into his foot-high black combat boots. He tried to hide the handcuffs under his orange windbreaker, but airline employees knew the signs of a prisoner in transit. His only luggage was a knotted garbage bag—and he was allowed to board first, even before children and wheelchair passengers.

According to a reporter who was aboard the plane, ''Mr. Graham sat on the back row between his escorts. The prisoner spent the flight sleeping, chatting sparingly with his guards, browsing computer ads in an airline magazine and struggling to sip a Coke and eat pretzels, with his wrists cuffed beneath a bulky nylon jacket. Much thinner and taller than his escorts, Mr. Graham was quickly recognized by fellow passengers and by flight attendants, who had been told only that they had a prisoner from the Fort Worth area. Toward the end of the flight, Mr. Graham declined to talk about his case, answering a request for comment with a smile and a polite shake of his head.''

As Tarrant County warrant officer Johnny Prince escorted Graham through an assembly of reporters and photographers in the underground parking lot of the justice center in Fort Worth that afternoon, *Dallas Morning News* reporter Selwyn Crawford shouted toward him, "Do you have anything to say to Diane?"

Graham, looked up and said softly, with a sheepish grin, "I love you."

Graham was escorted upstairs to await his formal arraignment, where he was ordered held on $100,000 bail. Booked in, he was issued a brown jail jumpsuit. After that, said Commander James Skidmore, head of the Tarrant County sheriff's department, which ran the jail, because of the intense publicity the case was receiving, Graham would be put in protective custody, otherwise known as solitary confinement. His fiancée was in the same building, said Skidmore, but the two wouldn't be visiting each other. They could write to each other, however. "That's their constitutional right," he said.

And write they did.

The day after Graham arrived at the detention facility, a jailer screening outgoing mail read a one-page letter Diane Zamora wrote to her fiancé. In it, she made several references to hurting herself, saying she banged her head on the bars of her cell at night, promising to continue to do it. "I could possibly die," she wrote.

Zamora was immediately removed from her cell and put on a suicide watch in another part of the building. "We handle situations like this every day," said Skidmore, who said she was checked every 30 minutes. Skidmore would not reveal the contents of the letter nor the intended recipient, but he did characterize what she had written, saying,

"I've done something, I've done something, and if I keep doing it, I could possibly die."

The jail's medical staff, however, could find no signs of self-inflicted wounds and a prison psychiatrist who examined Zamora the following day pronounced her nonsuicidal. She was back in her solitary confinement cell before the next news cycle began.

Diane's mother Gloria visited her daughter and pronounced her "innocent." Said Gloria: "She wanted us to be proud of her. She wanted everyone to be proud of her." Gloria said that her daughter was a religious person and was reading the Bible in her jail cell. "These are two young kids," she added. "They've never, ever done anything wrong."

Word of her having known about the murder for months had not yet gotten to the press. "We are coping OK," said Gloria. "We believe in our faith and we know. He has give us supernatural strength to see us through. I know Diane is innocent. She's a good kid."

But within two months, someone leaked word about Diane's having told her family of the murder. In a copyrighted story, the *Dallas Morning News* quoted sources "familiar with the case" who said that "the Zamora family held a prayer meeting soon afterward at which Ms. Zamora was 'forgiven' for the crime."

Led by her grandfather, pastor Mike Mendoza, Diane's parents and grandparents gathered around the young woman, prayed for her and asked for God's forgiveness.

Then, said one of the sources quoted by the paper, "They told her that [the murder] was in her 'old life,' and this was her 'new life.' "

If true, this would have meant that not only Zamora and Graham—but also Zamora's family and perhaps at least one friend—stood by while Bryan McMillen went to jail.

Zamora's attorney was quick to deny that such a family gathering ever happened. "The prayer meeting unequivocally did not occur," said Linebarger. "I've had a million meetings with those people and they've never mentioned that to me."

Sylvia Gonzalez, a frequent family spokesman after the arrests, also denied the allegation. "We didn't know anything about what happened. None of the family knew. It never happened. The family did not know anything about the murder, or Diane's part in it, until after she was arrested.

"We are a normal family, like anybody else," she said. "The only difference is we got involved in this because of Diane and we didn't choose to."

But in addition to the two anonymous sources the paper cited for its information, the Dallas paper also quoted Diane's Annapolis friend Jay Guild, saying, "I know that she told her mom about it. She told me [that] she told her" just after the killing.

Mike Parrish, meanwhile, flew to Colorado Springs and to Annapolis, on evidence-gathering missions. He claimed he was having a difficult time getting witnesses to cooperate with the grand jury.

What should have been an open-and-shut case—with two confessions and plenty of evidence—was turning hard. If the confessions were ruled inadmissible, could the gun and the barbells be ruled the result of an illegal search? And no witnesses?

Or was it a ploy? How many witnesses to this killing could there be?

Parrish wouldn't say who wasn't cooperating. "Maybe they're friends, maybe they're family members," he said.

"A suggestion by Parrish that people aren't cooperating would lead me to believe that he is trying to get one of the targets to cooperate," guessed Dan Cogdell. "And it's not my client, so by deduction it's Zamora."

Linebarger wasn't talking. But most court observers guessed that the D.A. would put a great deal of effort toward convincing Diane Zamora to save herself by testifying against David Graham.

Finally, on November 11, 1996, well ahead of the deadline, Tarrant County district attorney Tim Curry delivered the indictments, charging Graham and Zamora with capital murder.

Both Graham and Zamora and their attorneys were in the courtroom to hear the reading of the indictments.

Except for their names, addresses, dates of birth and case numbers—Diane was number 0632829; David, number 0632999—the indictments were exactly the same.

"In the name and by authority of the State of Texas," Graham began, *"the Grand Jurors of*

Tarrant County, Texas, duly elected, tried, em-
paneled, sworn and charged to inquire of of-
fenses committed in Tarrant County, in the
State of Texas, upon their oaths do present in
and to the Criminal District Court, No. 4 of
said County that David Christopher Graham
hereinafter called Defendant, in the County of
Tarrant and State aforesaid, on or about the
4th day of December 1995, did then and there
intentionally cause the death of an individual,
Adrianne Jones, by shooting her with a deadly
weapon, to-wit: a firearm, and the said defen-
dant was then and there in the course of com-
mitting or attempting to commit the offense of
kidnapping of Adrianne Jones."

The indictment against Diane read exactly the
same. There was no distinction made between who
wielded the weights and who pulled the trigger. And
it was clear that prosecutors were able to convince
grand jurors that Graham and Zamora had kidnapped Adrianne, one of the prerequisites for charging capital murder.

As the capital murder law required, each defendant was also charged with "the offense of obstruction or retaliation." This, explained Parrish, was a
"don't-kill-the-witness rule" that was justified in
this case because "Adrianne Jones escaped from
them briefly. They had the option to leave her alive.
They chose not to."

The crime, the indictments ended, was committed
"against the peace and dignity of the state."

The indictments were shocking only in their simplicity. The two honor students, pride of their families, schools, towns, had been reduced to the status of white male and white female, "hereinafter called Defendant." So recently feted for their brilliance, honor and integrity, Diane and David were now identified by indictment numbers 0632899 and 0632999 and two stark words: capital murder.

If there was any good news for the fallen cadets in the indictment, it was that they would not die for their deed if convicted. Parrish had decided not to seek the death penalty. In some respects, it was a small bone. Graham and Zamora would receive mandatory life sentences if convicted of the capital murder charge. That meant they would probably spend 40 years behind bars—with no credit for good behavior. Though spared death, they could count on missing the most productive years of their lives, not rising through the ranks of the Air Force or Navy, not going to the moon as an astronaut or swooping onto the deck of an aircraft carrier, not getting married, not raising children, much less seeing grandchildren. They might emerge from captivity, assuming they survived, but with just enough free time to die.

"Of course I'm relieved," said Dan Cogdell. "Any time even the possibility of a death sentence exists in the courtroom, it frightens the backbone out of any lawyer."

But he claimed no surprise at the decision.

"We expected both of these—the indictment and the decision not to seek the death penalty," continued Cogdell, who felt that a death penalty was never "in the code of appropriateness."

Even Parrish conceded that the death penalty would have been difficult to seek for two teenagers who had absolutely no criminal history; were not, except in this one instant, flames of congenital depravity that jurors would relish extinguishing. Parrish also admitted that, for the purposes of obtaining a death sentence, it was unfortunate that Adrianne Jones, as heinous as her death was, knew David Graham. Jurors were more likely to hand out a death sentence if the killer didn't know his victim—a "cold-blooded" execution, in the idiom of nonjuridical emotions, instead of a "crime of passion" spooked from a jealous lover—the latter could leave a residue of understanding in the minds of some jurors, enough empathy, perhaps, to spare the killer's life. It was easier for jurors to reward a ruthless and unfeeling butcher with death than to execute a lovestruck honor student.

Parrish was not conceding anything, however, except the realities of presenting the case to a jury. In fact, he said, "This was not a spur-of-the-moment situation. They talked it over with each other, they planned it out, they discussed how to do it. . . . They are bright, very bright. They know how to plan, think and kill."

Cogdell later responded, "I believe my client is bright. He is articulate. He is an accomplished individual. He is not capable of planning out an execution.

"My client is still focusing on the guilt-innocence phase of this—not punishment," said Cogdell, who nevertheless remained confident that his client would walk.

"I don't think there's any case with respect to David Graham," he said. "I do not believe that a rational jury could ever convict David Graham of kidnapping. That is a stretch beyond all imagination."

But even if Parrish could not make the kidnapping charge stick, it did not mean the defendants would walk. If a judge decided, at the end of the evidentiary stage of the trial, that capital murder was not justified, he had the option of allowing the jury to find the defendants guilty of a "lesser included offense," including simple murder or even manslaughter. Under those circumstances, few believed that Graham or Zamora would be free anytime soon.

Parrish said that there were several reasons for not seeking the death penalty, "but one of the main reasons is that after visiting with Bill and Linda Jones many times . . . their desire is that these two murderers spend a life sentence in the penitentiary."

Though perhaps there was some vengeful wrath at work in their desire to see the two waste away their lives in prison, Parrish suggested that it was compassion that prompted the Joneses to ask the prosecutor not to seek death.

"They know what it's like to lose a child," he explained, "the anguish and the pain of going through life without them every day. They don't want either of these suspects' parents to go through that."

"Everything's coming to a head like it's supposed to," Linda Jones told Deanna Boyd of the *Fort Worth Star Telegram.* She was sympathetic with Carlos and Gloria Zamora as well as Janice and Jerry Graham. "They didn't raise their children to be like this. No one does."

Linebarger called the Jones family decision "admirable."

But Linda Jones expressed no special compassion for her daughter's indicted killers. "I want them to get the maximum sentence available, and when it's time for parole, we'll wish them no luck. They don't need to be out. They need to pay the consequences of their crime."

Meanwhile, both attorneys had a problem on their hands: their clients kept talking. Mostly, it was by letter. But the intercepted "suicide" note was a worrisome sign that Graham and Zamora would continue to communicate, beyond the reach of an attorney's counsel.

Linebarger admitted his frustration in trying to muzzle Diane. "I don't think I can control that," he said of her letter-writing. "I've told her and told her and told her, 'Don't do it.' But they're still, as far as she's concerned, the ultimate couple. They still think they're going to get married."

Cogdell seemed more resigned to the communications. "I would prefer that he not talk to anyone on the planet," Cogdell said. "But that isn't realistically possible. So I have told him not to discuss the facts of the case with anyone, and that includes

Ms. Zamora.'' And whatever he wrote, Cogdell explained, he told Graham to make certain that what he wrote was accurate. "If he understands that,'' said Cogdell, "then those letters are harmless.''

Jay Green had been watching the news till he was almost numb. He saw his best friend, his "brother,'' being led to jail, saw Graham's picture on the front pages of newspapers and magazines and was angry, sad, confused. He wasn't sure exactly what to feel. He had a dream in which he came up to Graham in a courtroom. "Graham, I'm so sorry,'' he told his friend in the dream. "I forgive you, man.'' Then he embraced Graham.

Less than a week after Graham's arrest, Jay Green was applauded at a banquet in which he received an award for being the most-decorated cadet in his school's Air Force Junior ROTC program. Afterward, he was approached by a *People* magazine reporter seeking an interview about Graham. Recalled the reporter, "he flashed an icy, name, rank, serial number look, and replied, 'No comments, sir. No comments.' ''

Police had already cleared Green of any involvement in the crime—or even knowledge of it. He was sickened by the thought of what his friend had done.

But a couple of weeks before Thanksgiving, still in the midst of his bewilderment, a small white envelope arrived in the mail. The return address was Tarrant County Jail, CID number #0460856. Green ripped it open and read hesitantly.

Dear J,

Well, pal, I'm not sure if this letter will ever reach you because I'm just going to have to guess at your address, and if your parents intercept this letter they might scan it or trash it for your well-being. I can't blame them; I might do the same. Attention Mr. and Mrs. Green: if you read this, please give this to your son. Thank you.

Hmm. Where do I start? Well, I guess I could say first of all not to believe ANYTHING you see or [crossed-out word] hear from the media, because they're full of CRAP!!! Second, I would've written sooner, but I haven't until now because I just wasn't sure how you'd react. I have to say, you were always one of my best friends, and I hope not to lose that friendship over this. The police told me that you gave them a statement and I wanted you to know that whatever you said was your duty as a citizen, and I don't hold it against you at all. This is important, because when I get out, I don't want you thinking I'm going to chase you down and beat the tar out of you or anything. On the other hand, I would rather come see you and catch up on things around Burleson, or wherever you may be. A third reason I'm writing you is you have some of my stuff! Ha! Ha! Don't sweat it—just hang on to all that junk for a while.

I am very optimistic about the trial as I have one of the nation's best attorneys working for me for next-to-nothing (my sister knew his wife). Hey, it pays to have connections. I'm not too sure what will happen in Diane's trial, but as I'm sure you know, we are still the same old Romeo and Juliet we ever were. Lately, she has been helping me stay optimistic by sending me plenty of cheerful letters and Biblical messages. I know you are a man of faith, so let me tell you, Mark 11:24 says that whatever things you ask for, you shall receive. Trust me, we've been praying. Like I said before, the news media is completely wrong and besides, God forgives people for anything anyway, right? Well, I'll let you form your own opinion about all this—it's your right. Just believe me when I say I need you as a friend now more than ever. If you care to write me, just find the return address on the front and copy it down. Make sure you include the number 0460856. If you care to write Diane, she would also appreciate a letter . . .

I guess that about concludes this letter. I hope you decide to write. I wish you the best of luck in your senior year at Burleson High and the Texas 801st. Say "Hi!" to Sarah H. for me, and you can give her my address if she wants it. I ran into her dad the first night I was here, and he's more friendly here than he was at his house before I got arrested! Strange, huh?

Well, I guess it's goodbye for now. I look for-
ward to seeing you in the future.

Still your friend,
David Graham

p.s.   *Heard from Joseph?*
       Tell his mom I wrote—give her
       my address if she wants it.

Green read through the tight-script, two-page letter unbelieving. Was this the same Graham he
knew? What did it mean not to believe anything he
read? That he didn't kill? And if not, why didn't he
say that? And if he did kill, there was no remorse
whatsoever.

The young cadet was angry that one of his best
friends would commit murder; worse, Graham offered no explanation—and little recognition—that
he had done anything wrong. Quite the opposite:
"God forgives people for anything anyway. . . ."
And he had the nerve to say he hoped they could
still be friends. It was as if he didn't know the letter
writer. And in fact, the letter was signed "David
Graham," as if it were from a stranger.

Green put the letter away, perplexed and dis-
gusted.

Linebarger seemed more concerned by the letters
his client was writing than Cogdell was about Graham's continued written confessionals. "They are
still in love," said Linebarger. "Obviously, I wish
they wouldn't do it, but they still have a First

Amendment in this country. I don't get to censor these letters. But the prosecutors get to see those letters.''

"I want to see David," Diane told Linebarger. "Then this thing will go away, and we'll raise a family.''

It was as if the murder, which held them together, had also not happened. They called it love. A life of fantasy powerful enough to propel Diane to great accomplishment, against many odds, she now invoked to shield her from the realities of prison.

"At the very beginning," explained Sylvia Gonzalez, "we were totally shocked and finally she started telling us, 'OK, look, this is what really happened, but I have to do this. You all don't understand our kind of love.' ''

The tantalizing hints of coverup were everywhere.

"Well, of course, we disagree," continued Gonzalez. "We told her it's a sick obsession, that's what it is. It's not love. What kind of love is it when he is willing to turn you in or have you take the blame too? That's not love.''

In a jailhouse letter to David, obtained by the *Dallas Morning News,* Diane seemed genuinely confused by her incarceration.

"My head replays the scene over and over," she wrote. "Each time, I try to explain to the court sensibly what happened, but they find me guilty anyway and sentence me to twenty years.''

John Linebarger knew that his client faced the possibility of spending far more than 20 years behind bars. Diane said in her letter that she was sorry that the murder had gotten in the way of David's plans. "The Academy was always your dream, and now I've just crushed it," she wrote, seeming to take the kind of responsibility for the murder that Graham had alluded to in his confession. "Now I want to kill myself."

"She's been trying to cover up and take care of David," Sylvia Gonzalez told the *Dallas Morning News*. "She seems to think they have this Romeo and Juliet–type relationship. We've been talking to her and trying to get her to come to her senses. But she doesn't pay attention."

Coming to her senses would mean, no one had to say, cooperating with prosecutors, turning in David Graham, cutting a deal, saving her skin.

Parrish would not admit to any dealing, and would admit to having seen only the Zamora letter that prompted the suicide precautions for Zamora. "I'm not interested in anything they've got to say unless it's about the case," he said. "Hopefully, though, someone in there is paying attention and if they come across something, we would use it."

Graham was settling in, taking mail-order college courses, "not overtly complaining about the conditions," according to his attorney.

Perhaps he recognized that those conditions were better than the ones provided Adrianne Jessica Jones.

Epilogue

NO LAST WORDS

"If their confessions stand up . . . and they're found guilty, it will appear that the same drive and determination that brought success in classrooms and on athletic fields led them to view Adrianne Jones as just another obstacle to what they wanted; another obstacle to be removed."

—Mark Thompson, *Time* magazine

A murder sends many ripples across the lake of life, shattering dreams and overturning accepted notions as it churns its way through press rooms, courtrooms and living rooms in places near and far from the scene of the crime. Suddenly, Linda Jones, a massage therapist at a beauty parlor in a small town, her husband, two sons, neighbors, friends, relatives—suddenly, all of them are victims of a crime.

One of the first casualties of Diane Zamora's arrest was her Annapolis friend Jay Guild, who resigned his Academy appointment on September 9, two days after she was jailed. Guild said he had violated the Naval Academy's code of honor by not turning Diane in.

Suzanne McKelvy, a housewife in Mansfield, picked almost at random by a national television news team to comment on the murder, found herself singing at a memorial service for Adrianne Jones, then trying to start a magazine dedicated to crime solving and victims' rights. "It's really not an option whether I'm going to do it or not," she said. "My experiences surrounding Adrianne Jones made it evident that it is a calling for me."

A year after Adrianne Jones's murder, two months after the arrests of Diane Zamora and David Graham, Bryan McMillen and his parents called a press conference to announce that they were suing the Grand Prairie police department and three of its officers for wrongful arrest and imprisonment "Gestapo tactics," was how Linda McMillen characterized the nighttime arrest of her son.

It happened just as some Grand Prairie officials had predicted: as soon as real suspects were arrested, McMillen sued.

There was dramatic witness-stand testimony from a sobbing Diane Zamora—she would disavow her confession (see the Appendix which follows this Epilogue) and denounce her lover—as she told a rapt courtroom how Graham manipulated her throughout their love affair and masterminded the grisly assassination of Jones, forcing Diane to help cover up the murder. But jurors didn't believe it. After listening to the evidence during a nationally televised, two-week proceeding in February of 1998, they deliberated for less than seven hours over two days before returning a guilty verdict.

David Graham's trial, which was moved to New Braunfels, more than 200 miles south of Fort Worth, in July of 1998, was lengthier if less dramatic. The defense team, which was able to use the Zamora trial to refine their own strategy, tried mightily to persuade jurors that Graham's typed confession was coerced and should be thrown out. But in the end, admitted Graham attorney Dan Cogdell, the jurors "believed it placed him at the scene and it placed him in some responsibility."

"It sealed the case," said prosecutor Mike Parrish of the confession.

Graham too was found guilty of murder.

Linda Jones, summoning a surreal courage in the face of her daughter's death, remained faithful to her request that prosecutors not seek the death penalty for Graham and Zamora, and both were sentenced to life in prison. "It's difficult to lose a child," said Jones. "But to see two other children die is pointless."

"There are not any winners in this case," said Zamora trial judge Joe Drago.

Both Zamora and Graham appealed their convictions; both were denied. The two former cadets are behind bars, with sentences that would keep them there until they are in their sixties.

This case is not over. And the tree at the high school soccer field, with the plaque proclaiming "Unity, Strength, Courage," continues to grow in honor of Adrianne Jones.

APPENDIX: IN HER OWN WORDS

Whether Diane Zamora slept or not that first night in jail is unknown. But it was only a few hours after having been booked on murder charges and put in a cell at the Grand Prairie Police Department, that she was escorted to a small second-floor cubicle and there confessed to killing Adrianne Jones. It took a little over an hour to write her chilling, four-page account:

I, Diane Michelle Zamora, am 18 years of age and I live at 3804 Royal Crest in Fort Worth, Texas. I am making this statement to Grand Prairie Police Department Detective Alan T. Patton, who, before he began questioning me, while I was under arrest, and before I began making this statement, warned me (1) that I have the right to remain silent and not make any statement at all, and (2) that any statement I may make may be used against me at trial (or trials) for the offense (or offenses) concerning which this statement is made, (3) that any statement I make may be used as evidence against me in court, (4) that I have the right to employ a lawyer to be present either before or during questioning, (5) that if I am unable to employ a lawyer I have the right to have a lawyer appointed without cost to me to counsel with me and to advise me before or during any questioning, (6) that I have the right to stop answering questions at any time and may stop this interview or the making of this statement at any time whether I have answered some questions or have made some statements or not.

I do not want to talk to a lawyer before or during the answering of any questions or the making of this statement. I do hereby knowingly and voluntarily waive and give up my above explained rights and I make the following voluntary statement of my own free will and without promises or offers of leniency or favors, and through no fear, coertion [sic] or threats of physical harm by any person (or persons) whomsoever.

I remember that night, I think November 4, 1995, when David showed up at my doorstep. He had just come back from Lubbock and he had this look in his eyes that was horrible. He looked so scared. He had this red stuffed animal dog in his hands. I could tell something was wrong but I figured he was just tired. So he wanted to stay and spend the night. A month later I was coming into my house with him and I was questioning him about past relationships because he always told me that I was his first real girlfriend. I thought that was kind of strange because most people have some kind of relationship of one kind or another. I remember he read off a list of names of girls that he had known or gone places with, that were kind of sig-

nificant. I will never forget him mentioning the name Adrianne because that name kind of stuck in my head. I guess I was asking a lot of questions. For some reason I felt like I needed to ask about Adrianne. He held back a lot and we just went inside my house.

We just decided to walk inside of the house because we had been sitting inside of the car. When we got inside we got into a big fight because, as always, he was trying to make me study for the SAT and I didn't want to. We fought for a while and at the end, when we stopped fighting and had calmed down, he just looked at me and said, "I have something to tell you that is really important." I kind of knew that he was going to tell me, just by the way he looked at me.

He told me, "You haven't been the only girl in my life." He said, "I have had sex with someone else before."

I just looked at him in shock and I asked did he mean he wasn't a virgin when he met me and he said he was. I think that made me feel even worse 'cause that mention [sic] that he lost his virginity to me but that he had been with someone else since. All I could do was question him and scream and blame myself for everything.

I remember reaching out for this big brass thing, this brass rod and aiming it, and aiming for him and trying to hit him because I was so upset. He took it away from [me] and tried to calm me down because I was screaming so hysterically. He was trying to protect himself from getting hurt but he was also trying to protect from hurting myself because I was kept ramming my head against the walls and when I was on the ground I kept ramming my head onto the floor and tried to crack my skull.

I just didn't want to live with what he had said to me. I felt like I had lost everything. My hand wasn't working the way it should, my family wasn't in the best financial state, and now he was telling me the one thing I prized more than anything else was taken away. I don't think I was thinking, in fact, I know I wasn't thinking. I screamed at him, "Kill her, kill her." He was just so scared that he wasn't about to say no to me. I was still banging my head against the floor.

All David wanted to do was make everything better. It seemed like him agreeing to do that was the only thing that calmed me down. David promised that he would do that and David never has broken a promise to me before.

On December 2, 1995, we spent basically the weekend trying to get a hold of Adrianne. Nothing was really premeditated because I think we were both acting in passion. I think we expected to get *caught really fast because we didn't spend much time thinking about what we were doing. The only time David planned anything was when he sat me down at his house for about five minutes to calm me down and throw stuff in his bag. The plan was for David to break her neck and sink her body to the bottom of Joe Pool Lake. About 12:30 a.m. on December 4, 1995, we were at his house. David had said he would meet Adrianne at about 12:30 a.m. so we were late. We were driving my green Mazda Protege. It seemed like David put together what he was going to do really quick because he really didn't have much time to think.*

The day prior he had spend more time calming me down than thinking about what he was going to do. I would wake up in the middle of the night with nightmares. I couldn't even look at his face because I had thought he was a different person. I had horrible pictures running through my head about what happened between him and Adrianne and they made me feel really sick. We met her at about 1:30 a.m. on December 4, 1995, at her house. David had called her at around 10:30 p.m. on December 3, and it was pre-arranged for her to come out. She had thought she was coming out so they could have sex again. She came out to the car and got in. I was in the trunk and David was driving.

I remember being real scared because at a time like when you kind of know what's happening, you really don't trust anyone. I remember wanting to turn back. I was afraid to move so I just laid [sic] still in the trunk. David later told me that he felt the same way, that he wanted to turn back and take her home, but he was afraid of what I would do or say if he turned back. David usually always has a gun of some sort with him all the time. I knew that he had the Macrov 9-millimeter with him. I also knew that he had the weights. I don't think we knew what we were really going to do. It was more like we were going to get out there and just do it. David never specified an exact location of where he was going because I don't think he even knew where he was going.

We picked up Adrianne at her house and we drove for about 15 or 20 minutes. There's a hatch in the back seat. You can let it down and it leads into the back seat from the trunk. David pulled over to the side of the road and Adrianne had already leaned her seat back and he started I guess pretending that he was going to kiss her, and he motioned for me to pull the hatch down. I remember getting out and seeing that and it made me all the more angry. I knew he didn't mean it but it just made a bunch of pictures run [in] my head again.

When she saw me she kind of freaked out. David held her down and said it's OK, we just want to talk to you. I think at that point I could kind of tell he didn't want to do anything. I asked Adrianne about she and David having sex and she said that she didn't enjoy it, that there was too much guilt. I guess it was the way she looked at me when she said it that made me so angry. Even now I can only remember her eyes, but not her face. I remember screaming at David all over again. All of it just became so real.

I think I got kind of hysterical and I screamed, "Just do it. Just do it." David just started wrestling with her basically and she was trying to get away from him. I remember being scared that she was going to hurt him and so I reached to the back where I knew the weights were on the ground to try to hit her with it. I missed. I was just too nervous and my hands were just shaking too much. Probably the third time I did hit her on the head with the weight. Things kind of calmed down real quick and I was still really scared.

I think the whole time the only thing going through my mind was what was I doing, but I knew that things had gone too far and I couldn't stop. Somehow stopping seemed scarier than going on.

David turned his back. I don't really remember why and she slipped out of the window and ran off. We started to follow her with the car but we didn't go far because she collapsed into a field on the side of the road. David jumped out of the car with his gun because he didn't want to leave someone there. They could say something against us. He started running after her but she collapsed before he got to her.

He ran back to the car and he said, "She's dead." I was just too scared and I said, "Are you sure? No, she's not."

I told him to shoot her. "She's not dead."

He was really panicky and he wanted to take off but he went back to where she was 'cause I told him to. He shot her twice in the head. He ran back and jumped into the car and drove off as quick as he could.

I remember the first words out of his mouth were, "I love you, baby. Do you believe me now?" I said "Yes, I believe you, I love you too." I said, "What have we done?" His reply was, "I don't know. I can't believe we just did that."

We drove off. The whole time I was pretty panicky. We both knew what we had done was wrong and we both regretted it. I don't think anything could compare to that fear and that horrible nauseous feeling that I had all week. We went to John Green's house. I took David

[sic] *clothes and cleaned up his clothes for him. I think we were afraid to look at each other and in some ways I think we were really afraid of each other. When I finished cleaning up his clothes we walked from the bathroom to John Green's bedroom and just stood there looking at each other for a while until I broke down crying because I was so scared, and we held each other and prayed that God would forgive us for what we had done. He drove me to my house on Gatlinberg and we pulled the car into the garage. There was blood in the car. David was too sick to clean up anything. He was really pale and sick to his stomach. He wouldn't even step back into that car for months because it was so horrible of a memory. So I cleaned it up while he was in the bedroom asleep.*

I told him just to go to sleep because he had gone into the bathroom to vomit. He said he was pretty sick to his stomach. I really don't remember what he did with the gun right away, but months later he hid it in the attic at his dad's house. He left the weights in my car. I remember later I told him to come sleep by the fire and so we both went out there and slept by the fire, the whole time thinking the police were going to come to the door and arrest us.

His father called that morning to make sure he was up so he could go to school. Up to that point I don't think either of us really thought she was dead. But his father asked David over the phone, "Did you hear about that girl from Mansfield that was killed?" After he said that we basically knew that she was dead. Those next weeks were horrible because I couldn't eat and neither could he. He was always really jittery and pale faced. We were both afraid that each day together would be our last.

I remember we went to church a lot, praying that God would forgive us and somehow put us at peace because we were living in fear. I know God has forgiven us. I spent a lot of time thinking after that. I would pray day and night that God would send me back so I [could] *change what had happened. I would often start crying and tell David, "She didn't have to die." I guess I was kind of obsessed with praying and hoped that God would answer my prayers and send me back to fix everything.*

In a lot of ways I wish I could have known her better. Everyone talked about how sweet she was and that's something I will never know. My only comfort was that everything that happens, happens for a reason and maybe that we didn't know what it was. But we hoped in time that we would find out because I don't see how all that pain could have a reason.